SEEKING GOOD WORK

Memoirs of a Priestly Pilgrim

Thomas E. Ambrogi

For Wayne,
with blessings!
Tom

Intentional Productions

SEEKING GOOD WORK: Memoirs of a Priestly Pilgrim

ISBN: 978-0-9916152-0-9

Copyright © 2014 Thomas E. Ambrogi

Cover Design: Paul K. Austad
Book Design: Paul K. Austad / pkaustad.com

Interior text set in ELECTRA LT

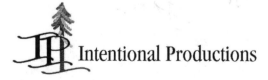

Intentional Productions

WWW.INTENTIONALPRODUCTIONS.COM

SEEKING GOOD WORK

Memoirs of a Priestly Pilgrim

Thomas E. Ambrogi

Contents

Prologue 1

Beginning the Journey 3
Transitions 8
The Early Jesuit Way of Life 14
The Georgetown Years 18
The European Years and Ordination 21
Ivory Coast and Ghana 32
Plunging Into the Ecumenical 34
Woodstock College Relocation 42
Lutheran and Episcopal Dialogue Groups 45
Moving On 50
Pilgrim Wife On the Journey 53
Israel, Palestine and the Middle East 58
My Wife the Lawyer 72
The Social Justice Commission 77
Ricardo Calderon 82
The End of the Affair 87
The Sanctuary Movement 90
To China 94
Stanford Dean of the Chapel 95
Food First 98
El Salvador 104
The Quakers 107
South Africa 110
Zambia and Zimbabwe 131
Pilgrims In Pilgrim Place 137

Slowly Settling In   140
Valuable Places to Be   143
My Magic Words   145
Our Festival   148
More Good Work   151
Back to South Africa   153
Again to China   155
Grieving Time   159
Another World Is Possible   164
D-Day In Normandy   169
Vietnam, Bangkok, and Cambodia   173
Out of the Forests of Paraguay   176
Teilhard de Chardin   181
The Terrible Tears of the World   185
The Later Years For Now   188

Postlude and Epilogue   195
Some Authors I Have Loved   199

Prologue

I was an active Jesuit priest until I was 39. All my earlier years had somehow fed into that priestly call, and all that has happened since then, now more than 40 years, has been shaped and formed by that experience. Along the way, I was blessed by knowing and loving many great people who did wonderful work, and I've been able to do some good work in their challenging and nourishing company.

I resigned my ecclesiastical ministry as priest in 1969, and as a wandering pilgrim around the world I have taught undergraduates and sought good work as a priestly person. My resignation was a life-changing event. I was no longer "Father Tom," and I suddenly had no history, no more networks or reputation, no more persona as priest in black suit and Roman collar.

There was a sting to the loss of status, of ancient relationships and community expectations, of a special life of honored service. It was a move from the center of the action to the margins, beginning to create my own narrative. A journey from the old to the very new.

That journey has taken me to San Francisco, Stanford, Stockton, Los Angeles and Claremont, to New York, Philadelphia, Washington, to Austria, France and Germany, to Ivory Coast and Ghana, to El Salvador and Guatemala and Nicaragua, to China and the Philippines, to South Africa for two years, and several times to Palestine-Israel. And now, since 1996, to the beloved ecumenical retirement community called Pilgrim Place, in Claremont, California.

Across this international zig-zag terrain of languages and cultures and social and political struggles, I have marvelous memories of a host of remarkable friends and gurus and co-workers. And, of course, central to it all has been the most wonderful gift of my life, my wife and companion on the journey for now more than forty years, Donna Myers Ambrogi.

The term "Good Work" means a great deal to me. It is that place where one's talents and enthusiasms can make a real difference in grappling with systemic change. That has always been the center of my search. I have often phrased it in the overriding question, *"Where is the valuable place to be?"* The term "vocation" was common, almost routine, in my religious life as a Jesuit. But Presbyterian theologian Frederick Buechner has stated the issue most powerfully: "Your vocation is that place where your deep gladness meets the world's great hunger."

There are no clear boundaries in the nomadic journey which follows here, but there will be an overall focus to it all, shifting through various time frames and from one central issue to another. I really have been a pilgrim person on the road. And by the unique sensitivity of God, the extraordinary ecumenical retirement community in Southern California to which Donna and I moved in 1996 is called *Pilgrim Place,* so the Spirit must be confirming something about my identity as wanderer and seeker.

Beginning the Journey

I was born in 1930 and grew up as the middle child of five, with an older brother and sister, Charlie and Agnes Marie, and two younger sisters, Joan and Patricia. It was altogether a very happy family. My mother was a beautiful, blue-eyed woman. Her name was Agnes, and her parents, of the Burke and McCarthy clans, had come from Killarney in the 1890s, and had settled in Scranton, Pennsylvania, where grandfather Burke worked in the coal mines.

I never knew my Burke grandparents, much to my great regret. But I have vivid memories of hearing how my mother's twin brothers, working as water boys in the mines, both died at age 8 in a mine disaster. I always had a strong bond to Scranton, where mother had grown up and where my brother and I went to camp every summer.

My father's name was Charlie, and he was a gentle man with a warm disposition and a shiny, balding pate. His parents came about 1890 to Ellis Island from Pisa and Lucca in Tuscany, and settled in Philadelphia, where they raised five children. My grandfather, who had the stunning name of Narciso Ambrogi, began his career in the land of promise by pushing a fruit cart on Dock Street in Philadelphia.

This cart later morphed into Ambrogi's Fancy Fruits, a very successful center-city up-scale caterer to fine hotels, now run by the third generation of my uncles and cousins. In my high school years, I happily worked there every Christmas packing and delivering gorgeous baskets of fruit.

In my grandmother's house in West Philadelphia, where the Ambrogi aunts and uncles would gather regularly for Sunday dinners, there was a lovely old wind-up Victrola and shelves of Red Seal records of the great Italian and Irish tenors, Enrico Caruso and John McCormack.

Some of my fondest memories as a young boy came from stories of how mustachioed Narciso, who was a very serious opera lover, would come home from pushing his

back: Agnes Marie, Patricia, Agnes (mother), Joan
front: Charlie, Tom. 1938

fruit cart on Dock Street, shower, gather his black opera cape and ebony opera cane, and head off with a flourish to the Opera House downtown. That ebony cane, with a large golden knob engraved with a rococo N-A, has been passed on for some years now, with fitting ceremony, to Narciso's grandsons and great-grandsons on their fiftieth birthdays. I had mine long ago, and it thrilled me to have it, even for a little while.

Although I was born in early 1930 in a large and sturdy home in Drexel Hill, in suburban Philadelphia, it occurs to me now that I had very little awareness that I was growing up in what was still the Great Depression. My father was the Treasurer of a thriving mill and mine supply company located downtown, and his job was apparently secure. Our street was filled with middle-class families and lots of us kids played ball in the streets and hiked about in a small woods at the end of the street, known to us simply as "the woods."

It was a happy place to grow up in, and I never knew anything different from that. I can move easily in memory through that lovely stone house today, especially up to the third floor attic room, where we had a live-in maid right off the boat from Ireland, named Rose Bradley. Rose had a mesmerizing brogue, loved each of us dearly, and would gather all five of us around her bed at night to play her accordion and lead us in all her Irish songs.

Other lasting memories of that house in Drexel Hill come from the war years starting in 1941 when my father was an Air Raid Warden, and my brother and I were Plane Spotters. We would walk around the streets and check during blackouts, and the whole family was called to "join the war effort" by food and gas rationing. In windows of the neighborhood were simple little flags, some with blue stars on a white background with red border, for family members serving in the military, or some with gold stars to commemorate a soldier killed in battle.

A very special friend next door, Charlie Beck, was an Air Force pilot who was shot down in a bombing raid over Germany, the land where his grandparents had been born. That was a very painful experience for his parents with whom we were very close, and Charlie was a handsome, beloved hero to us kids and to the whole neighborhood.

We were very happily involved with the local Catholic parish, and my brother and I were altar boys there. I vividly remember that we used to ride our bicycles, often in the morning dark, three miles up a long hill to Sacred Heart Church in sleepy Manoa, to be altar boys at the seven o'clock mass. The pastor, Father John Hickey, was a warm and beautiful man, and he was a great hero to us. He loved our family very much, and he was a strong and peaceful presence during our times of painful sickness and death, so he was a part of our family in a way that still moves me deeply.

We all had very warm relationships with the Immaculate Heart Sisters who taught all five of us in the parochial school, and then my sisters in high school and college. A number of those wonderful women had a powerful influence on my growing into a mature Christian faith, and I remember them all with gratitude and love.

As one of five young children, it was understood that I would responsibly work at something to take care of my own pocket money as a teenager, so I became a master landscape gardener in our neighborhood, with a whole list of customers whose lawns I would cut—for seventy-five cents, I somehow remember. I also remember making good money, for a kid, shoveling sidewalks. Then Charlie and I would do belly-flops in the street on our shiny Flexible Flyer sleds.

For several years in high school, I was also a bagger in the local A&P grocery store, and I enjoyed the prestige I earned among other teenagers from that. Managing my own budget helped me with the fair amount of dating I did in those years. I fell in love with a beautiful young brunette down the street, and we were a wonderful group of teens who found various great things to do together, including lots of dances within the local parish protectorate. I was even elected Best Dancer in my Senior Year in high school.

An enriching adventure of my teen years was becoming a Sea Scout, rather than the more usual Boy Scout. It was just at the end of World War II, and I liked the idea of wearing Navy sailor's whites and blues, with flashy bell-bottom trousers, bought with pride at the local Army and Navy Store. We had a Sea Scout base down in New Jersey on the Rancocas River, where we would go on Fridays to row our large, twelve-oar cutters and sail our small boats for the weekend, camping out on the sand.

We would hitchhike down to the base from Philadelphia, and in our sailor whites, people would think we were Navy men when they picked us up, which always made for some good conversations. It was all a great experience, in making good friends and learning the discipline and lore of sailing and knot-tying and seamanship.

Transitions

The Jesuit Order, the Society of Jesus, has played a unique role in my journey. My introduction to the Jesuits began in 1943 when I began commuting downtown to St. Joseph's Prep School, an hour by bus and subway. It was a classical Jesuit education with a strong Latin and Greek center that I enjoyed immensely. I was on the debating team, worked on the Yearbook, and was moderately athletic. In the school courtyard there was a place where everybody would play softball at recess time, and I did that regularly with gusto.

I got very enthused about rowing on the Schuylkill River, and was fascinated to work out on the Prep rowing team for a while. And then I became the manager of the basketball team for two years, a challenge I much enjoyed. We were statewide basketball champions, and when we were on the road all over the state, it was I who made sure that all the equipment was there as the team went out on the court.

I liked most of my many Jesuit teachers, but I became very attached to one of the priests, Ed Gannon, who turned into an ideal of major proportions for me. He taught English literature with great style and played jazz piano, was very bright and witty, very unclerical, and was idolized by teenagers for his sense of humor and his insight into young people.

Father Gannon also grew very close to mother and our whole family in the difficult times of death in our house during those years. Neither he nor anyone else ever sat me down to talk with me about my becoming a priest, but in my senior year I began to feel that I would like to be part of this Jesuit crowd of interesting men whom I admired immensely.

I admired particularly the diversity of things that Jesuits did. I guess most attractive of all, they were not at all churchy. They had broad spiritual and worldly interests, and were very articulate in their bright energy and obvious competence. They had a broad range of involvements in politics and in social justice work and in foreign missions and in the academic world.

I knew there were Jesuit universities and high schools all over the country and the world, and it was becoming clear that I did want to teach. Ed Gannon helped me into that conviction because I liked what I could see he was doing with his life with young people. I thought I might be able to have a similar kind of influence on young people, and that excited me. I grieved when he died in 1986, and I dearly treasure his memory.

So when I graduated in 1947 at age seventeen, I went off to the Jesuit Novitiate in Wernersville, Pennsylvania, fifty miles away in a fascinating Pennsylvania Dutch part of the world with horse-drawn Amish carriages clip-clopping down quiet country roads. I was there for four years, two years in spiritual formation as a Novice, and then two years as a "Junior," completing the first two years of my undergraduate college program there.

Without being at all gloomy, but rather just deeply real, death had been a constant companion in our home through all of my teen years. When I was fifteen and a high school sophomore in 1945, my father died of a coronary at age 47, in his own bed upstairs with all of us, his wife and five children, holding hands around him. Mother had nursed him there for over a year, with whatever help we could offer, so his dying was an extraordinary family experience.

Then, three years later when I was eighteen and a Jesuit Novice, my mother died of breast cancer at age 46. My brother Charlie was just twenty-one, and a U.S. Navy recruit serving in Guantanamo Bay, Cuba. My older sister, Agnes Marie, was twenty and a college sophomore, and the two younger girls, Joan and Patricia, were about twelve and seven. By special privilege not usual for a Jesuit Novice in those days, I was allowed to come home from the Novitiate to spend the last four weeks around mother's death-bed in the hospital.

So once again, we found ourselves deep in the experience of family death, and that came home to us most powerfully on the night of mother's wake in our living room, when a long line of family friends came in the driving rain of evening to pay their respects to the five of us kids standing beside the casket of our mother. That whole rich experience shaped us into a warmly coherent family for many decades to come.

After about a week of gathering our wits as a family

of now five, Charlie drove me back to the Novitiate in
Wernersville, and I still can summon up that event as
if it were yesterday. It was four o'clock in the afternoon,
and the long, marble corridors of the huge building were
totally quiet as all of the 200 Novices were in their rooms
for Afternoon Meditation.

I wanted to see our Master of Novices, Father John
McAvoy, a warmly humble and deeply spiritual guru
with whom I had already shared much of my soul for a
year. But his door was open and I didn't know where he
might be. I stood there all by myself and looked down
the long corridor at the shimmering brilliance of the sun
setting across the marble, and I started to cry. I slid down
the wall and sat there on my haunches, silently crying to
myself for some time.

I have come to realize that this was a uniquely for-
mative event in my overall growth as a person. At that
moment, I recognized for the first time that I was now
an orphan, at age 18. I didn't have a mother and a father
anymore. They had been gently beautiful and nurturing
parents who loved me dearly, and whom I dearly loved,
but now I was on my own, and whatever I would make of
myself would have to be on my own power.

That experience has stayed vividly with me, and I
think it has had a lot to do with my being a lone rider, always riding light in my saddle in regard to all the borders
and institutions and situations around me.

Not long after mother died, family discussions began
about what should be done with our lovely home in
Drexel Hill. When I went back to the Novitiate after the

funeral, Agnes Marie was a college sophomore, and she agreed to continue keeping the house going—quite a wonderful commitment as I now look back on it.

Charlie had to return to the Navy for a year or two, and the younger girls were in school and living at home. When Charlie decided to get married, and Agnes Marie was considering the same, the big question of whether we should sell the family house had to be faced.

I was, of course, the Wise One in the seminary, who was presumed to have special spiritual resources to settle this challenging decision, so letters from all sides began to arrive at my contemplative door. I prayed a lot about it, and I finally wrote back that, as they began splitting up to form their own new families, the unitary family we had been for decades simply was no longer, and the house was now the symbol of a family that had evolved into something new, a network of families instead of a single-family community. It was time to sell the house. That word from the cloister seemed to bring enough clarity, and the difficult decision went ahead.

Giving up the house became for me another personal metaphor of moving on. As the family arguments came in, I remember so well that their biggest stumbling block was that "if we sell the house, Tommy won't have any home to come home to."

Just at that time I was still deepening my awareness that I was an orphan, and now I would have no house and no family to come home to. In these realities of house and family, I find deep roots for what has become a major guiding theme of my pilgrim journey.

I later learned that Ignatius Loyola, founder of the
Jesuits, set out on pilgrimage from his family home in
search of God's will in his life. When he dictated his
autobiography toward the end of his life, Ignatius still
referred to himself as the "pilgrim." I, too, am a pilgrim
on the way.

And even though I would not have used the word
pilgrim in those years, I have all my life been on the
road, with no stopping place and open for new directions
at the next bend in the road. To reinforce that reality, all
four of my siblings have now died at relatively early ages
from various cardiac and cancer causes, so that for the
last nearly fifteen years, and now 84, I have been the lone
rider from among our original family of seven.

I have recently discovered another important reality
about losing my parents at age 18. All around me here in
the Pilgrim Place community today, I hear friends talk
about relating to their grown children with those children's unique exploits and problems, and I feel personally
and spiritually deprived that I was never able to relate to
my parents as an adult person myself.

Not much else to say about that except that I wish
it had been otherwise, and then I recall that wonderful
saying that "hope is giving up on ever having a better
past." There is something special in me that should be
being expressed by my experience with death. Among
many other things, I take it to mean a great deal about
how I treasure my dear wife and the friends I make, and
how important they are to me.

The Early Jesuit Way of Life

When Ignatius Loyola founded the Society of Jesus in 1540, its uniqueness was that it was not to be a contemplative, or monastic, community, as were the Benedictines or the Franciscans or so many other religious orders. Jesuits are rather called to be "contemplatives in action." They don't withdraw into a monastery to find God and then go out to serve the world. The challenge is to find God in all things. One doesn't bring God to the world. One goes into the world and uncovers—or discovers—the presence of God already there.

In all their ministries, the first call for Jesuits is to employ their intellectual talents, resources, time and energy in service as agents of social justice and human rights and transformative change *in* the world. As a first-year novice, I learned all this in great depth and with great excitement during the "Long Retreat," a thirty-day silent and solitary immersion into the Spiritual Exercises of Ignatius, which was led by a holy and remarkably perceptive Retreat Master, and was meant to probe whether I had a vocation to this way of life. One day a week we would be free to hike, although still in silence, in the woods and hills around the house.

After two years as a Novice, I took perpetual vows of poverty, chastity and obedience, and thereby became a full member of the Society of Jesus. Even though I have today been ecclesiastically dispensed from those vows, I still look upon poverty, chastity and obedience as being, in the light of Jesus' own example, not sacrificial burdens or disciplines but continuing signals for myself of a committed life, built on availability, simplicity and service.

Still at Wernersville, I then moved across the house to the "Juniorate," where we would have two years of classical studies leading to a bachelor's degree in the Humanities. That humanistic education, almost medieval in its rich classical structures and disciplines, became the background for nearly everything I later did in the academic world, even when I moved beyond Classics into teaching philosophy and literature and then theology and politics.

Every Monday evening from 7 - 9 PM, in our tiny, curtained rooms down the long marble corridors, we would each be writing a three-page "theme," in Latin and on any topic of our choice, later to be corrected by our professor, Fr. John Creaghan, who had just finished, awesomely for us, his Ph.D. in Classics at Princeton.

In the large dining room in the house, seating maybe 200 men in their cassocks, every evening there would be first a scripture reading from a large pulpit, followed by selections from some good current literature during the meal, which was in silence except on special occasions. From time to time students would preach a sermon there to practice their rhetorical skills.

I was among the better students, and I once was chosen for the great honor of preaching a sermon in classical Greek during the evening meal. I can't quite believe today that I really did that, preaching in Greek about St. Athanasius the Great, with everyone munching and slurping their soup in silence before me. But I do have a copy of it in my files, painstakingly typed on a Greek typewriter that I borrowed, just so that I would be sure to remember.

The normal Jesuit course brought me next to three years of concentrated philosophy studies, and I moved for that to Plattsburgh, New York, where the order had just bought the large old Hotel Champlain, sitting high on a bluff looking out over Lake Champlain, six miles across to Burlington, Vermont, and not far north from there to Montreal.

From October to April we lived in a wonderland under ten feet of snow, and the lake would freeze three feet thick. We would skate and sled and fish through holes drilled in the ice until, with bets being placed all around the lake on the exact moment of its timing, the ice finally cracked straight across with a resounding roar and hissing steam on an exciting day in early spring. It was a fantastically beautiful little wonderland of its own, and I still look back on it with delight.

Alongside my very exciting philosophical adventures, I received one of my most precious lifetime blessings in those years, a gift from a devoted professor. In my third year, I wrote a 150-page Master's thesis on *"The Historiography of Herodotus."* When I turned it in to my Classics professor, Fr. Creaghan, I didn't hear a word from him for a long time. We kept passing one another in the hall, and finally, he called me into his room and handed me my manuscript, all marked up and scribbled over in red ink.

"Don't be discouraged," he said to me. "This thesis is really very good, and I think it could be even better, which is why I spent so much time on it. Now I invite you

Preparing for Priesthood, Plattsburg, New York, 1953

to write it out by hand in pencil, all 150 pages. Wherever you see that I suggest another phrase or expression than yours, think about it and change it in your own pencil script if you think it's better, and don't be afraid to erase that if you come back later and decide that your own expression was in fact better."

I very carefully did that, and when I had finished it in several weeks, I recognized that this dear man had taught me how to write the English language. I still have that handwritten pencil script in my files. Whatever college course I later taught, on whatever subject, in the next forty or fifty years, besides the content of the course I always made it a major priority to help my students write the English language well, and I have spent a great deal of my time and energy taking their writing seriously, because of that gracious gift that my Classics professor had given me long years earlier.

The Georgetown Years

In those three years on Lake Champlain, I completed an M.A. in Classics from Fordham University. I was then appointed an Assistant Professor in Classical Languages and Literature at Georgetown University in Washington for three years, 1954-57, where I switched gears into a broader and richer world than ever before.

Washington was a very exciting city in those years, and through several Jesuit colleagues who were teaching in the Georgetown School of Foreign Service, I found myself making the rounds of gala receptions and international events in embassies all around the city.

It was a great challenge to live with forty freshmen in a men's dormitory on the quadrangle of the campus. Though only a few years older than those students, I was prefect of the residence hall, which meant not only keeping discipline, but also being counselor, academic tutor, spiritual director, and all-round good guy and guru for each of them, as well as for all their girl friends from neighboring colleges. In those years, I had a piled-high head of blond hair—hard to believe today with my balding pate—and that gave rise to the students' nickname for me, "Ambrogi, The Golden Guinea."

I tremendously enjoyed teaching four Classics courses, two broadly surveying classical literature in English, and then two in the original Greek and Latin texts. Among other things, we read all of the Iliad and the Odyssey, and also Vergil's *Aeneid,* as well as Greek and Roman history and literature and poetry, all in the original. We also read Plato and Aristotle and the Greek rhetoricians.

Among the very bright students who sat breathlessly at my feet in those days were Antonin Scalia and Patrick J. Buchanan, but I'm always somewhat hesitant about mentioning that in mixed company. Every time I hear Scalia orate, I think of the time I spent reading Demosthenes with him, and wonder how I ever could have taught him all that bombast.

I regularly put together a small group of students who would personally become proficient in reading the twelve books of the *Aeneid* in the original, and we had what we called the Vergilian Academy.

Every year, I invited three Classics professors from top universities around the country to come for a "Grand Act," as the Europeans would call it, where four prized students were quizzed by a panel of professors for three hours on the Latin text of the *Aeneid,* before a large crowd of professors and students in Gaston Hall, the Great Hall of the University. It was a very formal and white-gloved occasion in the best academic tradition.

It was a delight for me a few years ago to get a letter from a former student, now a retired Dartmouth philosophy professor living in New Hampshire, who said he had been in the Academy, and that he still treasured a signed copy of the *Aeneid* which I had given him in 1957.

I was also delighted to hear that a new Pilgrim Place resident, Darlene Nicgorski, has a brother, Walter, whom I remember well as a very bright student in those Classics adventures. Walter has become quite a Cicero scholar, has published a great deal, and has just retired after a remarkable career in the Humanities Department at the University of Notre Dame. Gives an old professor quite a kick to hear such stories.

It is astounding for me now to realize how personally apolitical I was in those days of the mid-fifties. Being immersed in my undergraduates and the thrill of my teaching and the international social buzz around Georgetown was an all-engrossing experience for me, and, though I loved the city of Washington and its cultural life, I was actually little involved in what was going on in the White House or on Capitol Hill. All the social and political issues that are my obsessions today—war, poverty, environment, racial and gender justice, militarism and the U.S. foreign policy of Empire—were realities only later to come onto my scope.

The European Years and Ordination

In the summer of 1957, I went off to Europe for my four years of Jesuit theology studies. I had asked my superiors to send me to the Sorbonne in Paris to study, since I loved everything French and I already knew some French from school. But then I got a call from my Provincial Superior, saying I would go to the University of Innsbruck, in Austria.

I really had to look up where Innsbruck was on a map. And when I cleared my throat and commented that I didn't know any German, he said, "Well, we know that, but this will give you a chance to learn some German." Such was the vow of Jesuit obedience in those days, and I boarded the Holland America's Nieuw Amsterdam and sailed off on the first of what would become my six transatlantic crossings.

While doing an intensive two-month German language course with the Goethe Institut in Blaubeuren, near Ulm in Baden-Württemberg, I came to live with a wonderful 85-year-old Oma and her two remarkable young granddaughters, Christa und Hiltrud.

I knew not a word of German, and they just a little English from school, and we had a great time while they taught "Pater Tomas" to repeat what he had just learned in his German class, with acting-out and just laughing a whole lot. These are all very dear memories for me, and after this brief but excellent language course, I was ready to head on to the University of Innsbruck for four years.

Austria in 1957 was just coming out of its tripartite

division by the Russian, British and American Allies after
World War II. The Jesuit College on the Sillgasse in
central Innsbruck had only recently been given back to
the Jesuits after having been commandeered for use as a
Nazi SS Headquarters in the Tirol.

It was a huge building, with long marble corridors
around a central courtyard, drab and gray and badly in
need of repair. I could still hear the clicking of heels and
ghostly German voices in the corridors, especially in the
tiny cells in the basement, and I could only imagine what
Nazi terror had played out there.

The Jesuit complex included a baroque University
Church, and the rambling residence itself could easily
hold the 250 Jesuits who came from around the world to
study in the Theological Faculty of the University down
the street. Like all of recovering Austria at the time,
we had very little money, and I remember well that the
menu for supper every evening for four years was nothing but dry bread, applesauce and water. Friends have
doubted my word, but that's how I remember it!

That's a lot of applesauce for 250 students every night,
and the apples were all dumped by big dump-trucks into
what used to be the coal-bins in the basement of the
building. We had heat and hot water in the house only
for a few hours three afternoons a week, so that for four
years I studied most of my theology bundled up at my
desk in my overcoat and hat and knitted muffler.

But all that became somehow manageable when we
had our free day from university lectures every Thursday,
to climb and to ski all over the Tirolean Alps just outside

Moving Toward Ordination, Innsbruck, Austria, 1957

our door. I thrived on the massive wonderland of beauty around me. The first order of business on arriving in Innsbruck was to climb up to a mountain village to get ski-boots and skis measured and made by hand, and then to learn to ski.

I got some skiing lessons from the Jesuit brethren, and on my first time down a huge mountain by myself, I remember taking a spectacular spill, head-over-skis. As I was dusting myself off and standing up, a very old Austrian man with a long beard and only one leg came zipping by on his one ski, tossing a wave and a Tirolean shout of encouragement for me. I could just about understand him, and it was a lesson in frustration and humility that is still fresh in my memory.

Renowned German theologian, Karl Rahner, was in his prime while I was in Innsbruck. These were the years shortly before the Second Vatican Council in Rome, in which Karl Rahner was to be a very powerful voice, even from Innsbruck over the Alps. Along with about 400 other students I would sit at his feet in the largest lecture hall in the University.

Rahner was exceptionally articulate and it took some time to get to understand his powerful and abstract German style, but it was worth every minute of that struggle. Karl's brother, Hugo—himself a beautiful man and a renowned theologian—used to teach Patristics at Innsbruck, and Hugo had famously said that he was going to spend his retirement translating his brother Karl's writings into readable German, so that ordinary folks might understand him.

Karl Rahner, who died in 1984, was an exciting polymath across many schools of theological and philosophical thinking. I got thoroughly immersed in his profound and stimulating vision of "Anthropological Theology" and his "Supernatural Existential." All of this resonated well with what I had seen of the post-war "Nouvelle Theologie" in France, as well as with Teilhard de Chardin's *Le Milieu Divin*, which had only recently appeared with world-wide acclaim.

Rahner's *Geist in Welt* was a worldwide best-seller, and my work with his whole synthesis of Spirit-in-the-World became my very welcome introduction, in later years, to both Liberation Theology and to Process Theology.

I fondly remember my Jesuit brother, Karl Rahner, as being a very dear man, which is wonderful to be able to say about someone of such renown. He was short and simple and slim, an exceptionally gentle friend, polite in the style of the warm, old-time German aristocracy. He was extremely bright and reserved, and was constantly "pondering imponderables" of many interesting kinds, even in the rarified theological world where he mostly lived.

A young American Jesuit who joined us had been a jazz drummer in an earlier incarnation in California. I remember that he gave a two-hour solo jazz drum concert on his trap-set one evening for the Jesuit community, rather wondrous for all of us Americans to behold and wildly applaud.

Karl was there in the front row, with furrowed brow in concentrated reflection as the concert proceeded, and we all laughed that he was now framing the theme for his next book, *"Das Wesen and die Entstehung des Jazztrommeln,"* or *"The Essence and Development of Jazz Drumming"* which we expected would be published in German and English, in three volumes.

Innsbruck was an exciting crossroads between East and West when I arrived in 1957. 1956 was, of course, the year of the Hungarian Revolution, and throngs of refugees from the East Zone were still streaming over the border and through Vienna. It was a powerful experience for me to go to the Innsbruck train station, which was just across the street, to watch the crowds of people searching the throngs coming off the trains from Vienna.

All over the station were signs and pictures held by men and women looking for their lost and wandering relatives and friends. "Here is my mother. Have you ever seen her?" And they would stay and sleep out on the floor of the station, quietly waiting for the next train's endless line of hopeful faces.

One day a young Hungarian knocked on the door of the Jesuit College, speaking Latin because he didn't know any German. He said he was a Jesuit seminarian and that a priest who had worked beside him in a factory in Budapest had been teaching him Theology on the assembly line for two years. Could he join us now to continue his Theology and be ordained?

Another decision soon came up, even more problematic, when a young German came to the door saying he had been a Jesuit before Hitler abolished the Order in Germany in 1939, and he wanted to come back. The Jesuit Order had been disbanded, with all its members scattered over Germany and beyond.

When these men suddenly appeared at the door, maybe after fifteen years of doing who knows what, before they were accepted back as a Jesuit it was a dicey but very important question to ask them where they had been and what they had done during the Nazi years of violence and repression.

These were difficult issues that were passionately discussed not just by our Jesuit superiors, who had to decide whether to take them in, but by our whole community of students as well. We did, of course, take them in, and we welcomed them warmly, if carefully, and we probed them for all the stories they could tell us.

One of my most memorable experiences was going in August of 1959 to Vienna for the World Youth Festival. The week-long Festival was the first of its kind since the Hungarian Revolution, and it brought together young people from around the world. Above all, it was the first time that groups of any kind were allowed to come from the East Zone to the "West," and I can still remember the fantastic excitement of it all.

Police guards nervously protected camps of Communist youth delegates from Poland and Czechoslovakia, from the Soviet Union and Hungary. It was only rarely that a friend and I were able to break through to some of those students to talk about what life was like for them. The rhythmic chant everywhere was "Frieden, Freundschaft," "Peace and Friendship," and I can still hear it ringing in my ears as I write. There were countless folk concerts and fireworks displays and discussion groups going on for a whole week around the Ring in the center of Vienna.

The climactic event of the week brought together 80,000 people (!) in a huge stadium, to watch folk dance groups from five nations, with the USSR being the last and the best. But a magnificent spectacle also came from 1200 Czech gymnasts   600 boys in yellow shirts and tan shorts, 600 girls in blue gym suits with white shoes. With fantastic precision and color on the bright green grass, they put on about thirty minutes of intricate choreography that must have taken months to practice. I remember writing in my journal that it was the most spectacular of spectaculars that I had ever seen, and I was sorry that Ed Sullivan could not have been there.

With a huge fireworks display, the 80,000 spectators then went home—the Poles, Czechs, Hungarians and Russians waiting until all was cleared before they safely could be moved from the stands. We followed them out and saw them bundled into their new grey busses and whisked away. "Poor kids," we ruefully muttered.

The Russian face was to me singularly non-expressive, often very glum and sober. There was much hand-waving and rhythmic chanting of "Frieden, Freund-schaft" as groups from other nations walked by to go out on the town. I still very warmly remember all this as the most profound international adventure I have ever had.

The next year, in the spring of 1960, I was ordained a priest in the baroque University Church in Innsbruck. "Finally, after thirteen years!" my family trumpeted as they sailed over from the States to share in the great celebration under the shining, snow-covered Alps. I lay prostrate on the sanctuary floor and had hands laid on me by the Austrian bishop, and I breathed a sigh of relief myself that the great day had finally come.

After proudly taking my family around a bit to my favorite haunts in the Tirol and Bavaria, I then continued with my fourth and final year of Theology in Innsbruck, helping out and learning to preach in German in Austrian parishes on Sunday mornings along the way. It was good work and my exciting introduction into being a pilgrim priest, and it set me on my way.

At the end of that year, I was due to take my final

comprehensive exam covering my whole ten-year Jesuit course of studies to that point, a three-hour public marathon open to anyone interested in coming to listen. We answered in German—or in Latin, if you couldn't understand the Hungarian or Slavic accent of the questioner's German. The matter under discussion was simply all the Philosophy and Theology I had ever studied, everything from my first year of Philosophy studies ten years earlier at Woodstock through these four years at Innsbruck.

We all were given a semester free to study and review for that monumental exam, and a unique opportunity came my way. The Rahner brothers' mother, Luise, well into her late eighties, lived in an Altersheim, or Old Folks Home, in Freiburg im Breisgau, in the Bavarian Black Forest. I was delighted that Karl was living there just at that time, rather than back home in Innsbruck, doing some writing.

So I arranged to get a room in the large house there, where I could both earn my way as a chaplain for the old folks and study in peace. Nearly every day for four months, Karl Rahner and I had breakfast together, and then we would walk together, pondering imponderables with our hands behind our backs (which was his way!) for more than an hour in the stately Black Forest. I remember it as a rich and very special time, and I even studied enough to pass the comprehensive exam at the end.

During this time, and for all the following four or five years I lived in Europe, I served as an Auxiliary Chaplain for the U.S. military, visiting the troops and celebrating Mass every weekend at a wide range of NATO and U.S.

Army and Air Force bases all over Germany and France and Belgium.

Besides the pastoral experience and satisfaction this gave me as a new priest, it was the only exposure I would ever have to the military way of life, since I had never been subject to the draft while in the Seminary. It kept me grounded in a special way, and helped me to form for later years many of my moral convictions about militarism, war and peace, and nonviolence, and my political awareness about our American policy of Empire.

The fifteenth year of the Jesuit course was called Tertianship, equivalently a third year of Noviceship, a year of spiritual theology, prayer and guided pastoral work designed to help us integrate all of our heady academic philosophy and theology with the realities of our spiritual lives as new priests.

For this, I was sent from Innsbruck to a French house in a small town in the Champagne, St. Martin d'Ablois, near Rheims. We were some fifteen international Jesuits gathered in a small house around another great priest and guru, Antoine Delchard, for a final year of "formation" and another 30-day "retreat of discernment" with the Ignatian Exercises.

After that very rich spiritual experience, building on my first Long Retreat as a Novice fifteen years earlier, I was sent out on a whole series of mentored pastoral assignments. I spent two months as a hospital chaplain in southern France, and then went to England for four months, where I preached and was a parish priest in Preston, in Lancashire. The local pastoral experience in both these places was very enriching, once I developed an ear for the rural French and the broad Lancashire accents of those I was working with.

During this time, I also continued to serve, whenever possible, as a Chaplain to the U.S. military in France and Germany, itself a wonderful experience and good work for a new priest. In all of this, which had a challenge all its own, I recognized that I was missing out on a lot of the political ferment of the 50s and 60s in the U.S. while I was away. In fact, I had really missed out on most of the civil rights movement and all that went with it.

The wonderful fifteen-year course of Jesuit studies instilled in me a love of silence which still frames the core of my spiritual life. I am in urgent need of quiet space, contemplative space, no matter what my activist self is doing or what is happening around me, and my recent reading in Buddhist studies now makes me grapple with the challenge of becoming a "Buddha Christian." That will certainly bring new excitement to my spiritual life, and I look forward to it with great anticipation.

When I had completed my last year in France in 1962, and with it my entire Jesuit course of studies of fifteen years, I was now a fully formed Jesuit. Then, by transatlantic phone, I was appointed to teach undergraduate Philosophy at Georgetown. I really had had enough of living with the French, who had become rather provincial for me by then, and it was time to go home, so that was fine.

But, once again, I told my Jesuit Provincial that I didn't really know much Philosophy. He replied again that he knew that, but that I had studied Philosophy in my seminary courses, and I should therefore know enough to teach it to undergraduates. The magic of Jesuit blind obedience again prevailed, and I was appointed Instructor in Philosophy at Georgetown University.

So I sailed home on Holland-America Lines and spent the year of 1962-63 back in Washington, living again in the dormitories, and enjoying very much the new courses on philosophical themes which I developed for myself and my undergraduates.

Ivory Coast and Ghana

In the summer of 1963, I got my first introduction to the continent of Africa, which would become a major focus of my interest in later years. Rev. James Robinson, the African American Baptist preacher who founded *Operation Crossroads Africa*, came through Georgetown and talked about his program of sending college seniors, and recent graduates, for a three-month mini-Peace Corps work experience in various countries of Africa.

Rev. Robinson said he had never had a priest lead a group for him, and I accepted his warm invitation to take full leadership responsibility for a three-month French-speaking Crossroads workcamp of twenty-five American and African male and female students in Ivory Coast, with some travel in Ghana to be included.

I organized the logistics of travel to and in Ivory Coast and Ghana, food and lodging, and liaison with African leaders on the details of a work-camp project to build a village school 300 kilometers into the rain forest in Ivory Coast. It was very hard work living in tents in the blistering sun, but we completed the little schoolhouse in three months, to our profound satisfaction. I admired Crossroads Africa immensely, and I later represented them at UNESCO conferences in Paris and Salzburg.

I was now 33 years old, had several graduate degrees and a broad humanistic and international education, but didn't yet have a doctoral degree in anything. So I spent a good part of the next year trying to decide what I wanted to be when I grew up.

I was still excited about teaching Classics, as I had done so enjoyably at Georgetown, so I wrote to a great hero of mine, Professor Gilbert Highet at Columbia, whose book, *The Classical Tradition*, had shaped me as a lover and teacher of Classical Literature. I asked him where he would go for doctoral studies today if he wanted to get the broad humanistic love and appreciation for classical literature which I so much admired in his own writing.

Gilbert Highet sent back a lengthy hand-written letter, which I still have, in which he said there was no longer any place where I could find such a degree program, except possibly an Oxon M.A. at Oxford, if I wanted to adapt that to my needs. Or I could go to Munich and try to create my own program somehow between the Philosophy and Literature faculties.

But all the best graduate Classics departments, Professor Highet said, are totally immersed in the auxiliary sciences of philology, linguistics, numismatics and archeology, and he didn't know where I could find a real concentration on developing a humanistic scholar specifically in classical literature, which is what I was seeking. This was exactly how I was seeing the graduate field of Classics, and his moving and very articulate response was a real challenge to me to re-think myself and my future in the academic world. I continue to be warmly grateful for his wisdom and his counsel.

Plunging Into the Ecumenical

After much prayer and soul-searching in the midst of teaching Philosophy to my Georgetown undergraduates, I finally decided in 1963 to do doctoral studies in Theology, originally with an eye to Ascetical Theology and Spiritual Direction, a career to which I was powerfully drawn at the time. But Gustave Weigel, my mentor and a Jesuit pioneer in ecumenism, convinced me to break out into what was then a new field, Ecumenical Theology, and my path was set toward becoming a profoundly ecumenical and interfaith Christian.

So I sailed back to France, again on Holland-America Lines. I chose the French-speaking University of Strasbourg for my doctoral work because it had both a Protestant and a Catholic faculty of Theology, not very common for a university in those days. I had long loved the beautiful city of Strasbourg, full of little Venetian-style canals and bridging French and German culture right on the Rhine River in Alsace-Lorraine. This was during the early years of Vatican II, and I plunged into exciting new courses in Protestant and Catholic Theology toward my degree in the University.

I lived as the only foreigner in a very small house of French Jesuits, right on a narrow, quiet canal. In my early time there, just fifty years ago, I have vivid memories of sitting all by myself watching the grainy, black-and-white TV account of President Kennedy's November 22, 1963 assassination in Dallas and the long train-ride of national grieving that followed it, with no one to share with me all my tears.

I also closed myself up for months at a time in northern Germany in a small ecumenical research institute, called the Johann Adam Möhler Institut, in Paderborn, in Westphalia. It was an ideal setting for writing my dissertation, in an efficient little house with six other doctoral students from various countries, a little kitchen, and a rich and sizeable library of Protestant and Catholic theology. I could write all week in academic silence and then go out on weekends to be my priestly self as a Chaplain to American troopers as they ran their tanks around on the plains of northern Germany.

My dissertation was entitled *"Positions doctrinales de l'Église luthérienne du Synode du Missouri: Étude oecuménique,"* or "Doctrinal Positions of the Lutheran Church-Missouri Synod: An Ecumenical Study." American Lutheran friends have often chided me that an ecumenical study of the very conservative Missouri Synod doctrine must have been rather thin; but that thesis, which I immensely enjoyed doing, launched me into broad ecumenical relationships that I still cherish.

The Lutheran Church-Missouri Synod began with a very conservative group of Germans who broke off from the Lutheran Church in Saxony in the 19th century. They insisted that they were the only "Martin Luther Lutherans" and they emigrated to the United States looking for "Zion on the Mississippi." Concordia Seminary in St. Louis continues that strong heritage today.

While my thesis was being read in Strasbourg in preparation for my defense of it before three international professors in a "Grande Acte" in the Great Hall of the University, I went down to Rome, with a stop in Geneva at the Lutheran World Federation, where I was warmly welcomed. "Here's an American Jesuit writing a thesis on Missouri," shouted the Director down the hall, and all the staff came out enthusiastically to meet me. This was really a brand new adventure at the time.

Although I had travelled very widely, I had intentionally never gone to Rome in my eight years in Europe, because I really was not sure that my faith could quite handle walking around there in my black soutane, which priests and religious had to wear on the streets in those days.

But now, it was exactly the end of the last session of Vatican II, and I spent all of my time with the large group of Protestant Observers at the Council. I particularly got to know Lutheran scholar George Lindbeck, from Yale Divinity School, and that became a warm friendship that lasted for many years thereafter.

I received my degree *Docteur ès Sciences Religieuses* (D.Sc.R.) from the University of Strasbourg in 1965 and was called to succeed Gustave Weigel in the new chair of Ecumenics at Woodstock College, the Jesuit School of Theology outside Baltimore.

So I sailed across the Atlantic for my sixth and final time, this time on the Italian Lines' Leonardo da Vinci, with all my worldly belongings in its hold, including my only copy of that precious doctoral thesis, which, hard as it is to imagine today, I had laboriously typed in French on a French typewriter, with a master and three carbon copies for the university.

On the sixth day out from Genoa, one day out from New York, the Leonardo came into a raging storm. Just at dinner time, with severe pitching of the massive ship, and dishes and wine glasses flying in the dining room, the Captain came on to announce that there had been a fire in the engine room, and one of the two turbines had burned out. We should all go back and strap ourselves into our bunks, and the ship was turning about and going back to Genoa, on half power and for another ten days at sea.

I still don't know how they did it, but there was enough food in their kitchens to feed us 1200 passengers for another ten days. From Genoa we were then all flown home on Alitalia. In a great test of my faith and hope, after several anxious weeks of living out of my suitcase, my steamer trunk was finally delivered to me at Woodstock by Alitalia Airlines, with that precious thesis and all my worldly belongings safe and sound.

It didn't take long to feel at home at Woodstock. It was very satisfying to really focus, for the first time, on Protestant Theology with bright Jesuit seminarians; and as an Assistant Professor of Theology and Ecumenics, I tried to fill the great shoes of Gustave Weigel. It was a blessing to do all that in the company of a stimulating faculty that included the brilliance of John Courtney Murray, among other very lively scholars.

Then, in late 1965, not long after I had gotten home, George Lindbeck called me from a faculty meeting at Yale Divinity School in New Haven. YDS was inviting Woodstock College, after almost 100 years in the "Woods and the Stocks," to relocate from Baltimore to New Haven in what would be a precedent-setting ecumenical consortium at Yale. I then spent several months in and out of New Haven, officially exploring that exciting possibility with the President of Yale, the Divinity School, and the Mayor of New Haven.

But the focus soon shifted to New York when John Bennett, then President of Union Theological Seminary, brokered an offer to bring Woodstock onto Morningside Heights in an even broader consortium with Union, Jewish Theological Seminary and Columbia University.

The ecumenical and interfaith possibilities of theological education then became the central passion and focus of all my teaching and academic commitments. While still teaching several courses at Woodstock in Baltimore, I commuted by train to an apartment at Union every week for almost a year, spinning out new models of contextual theological education and negotiating possible library, classroom and residence space for 250 Jesuit students all over Manhattan.

The vision was to re-fashion a traditional Jesuit community, where for centuries everyone had lived under one roof in the countryside, for safety from the world, and would stream to meals in silence in a long black line. We would now put all those energetic future priests into different small communities around the Greater Metropolitan New York area, coming together on Morningside Heights for a new kind of ecumenical and interfaith theological experience.

In the second semester, I was invited by Claude Welch, Chair of the Department of Religious Thought at the University of Pennsylvania, to stop off on my way through Philadelphia to teach a Graduate Seminar on Vatican II at Penn. I was a bit breathless at times, but I managed what became a very challenging commute between Manhattan, Philadelphia and Baltimore.

In early 1966, I got a phone call from Karl Rahner in Innsbruck, saying he had been invited to come to the University of Notre Dame to speak at a large conference on Vatican II, the first such event in this country since the Council had just ended in Rome. He said he had never been to the States, and asked if I would translate for him and show him around at the Notre Dame conference.

I was delighted, and that conference held a special blessing for me, since it was there that I first met Donna Myers, a member of the International Grail Movement who was editing an avant-garde monthly journal called

"Ecumenical Notes" and teaching at Alma College, the Jesuit School of Theology in Los Gatos, California.

Among many other things about Donna's charm, I was intrigued to meet the first woman ever to teach inside an all-male Jesuit seminary since the time of Ignatius. I only had a brief visit with her while taking Rahner about, and I didn't see her again for three years, but our meeting there turned out to be more promising than I could ever imagine.

While I was teaching Ecumenics and Sacramental Theology at Woodstock in 1967, I was invited to give the keynote address at the annual meeting of the National Liturgical Conference, to be held in the huge Cow Palace in Kansas City, with about 5,000 people attending.

Working from the outstanding document of Vatican II, "The Constitution on the Sacred Liturgy," I was asked to write and demonstrate a "Mass of the Future." What would the liturgical revolution of the new Council concretely look like around the altar? Looking back now almost forty years later, that "Mass of the Future" was a great challenge, even great fun to do.

The Cow Palace is enormous, and I felt like Billy Graham preaching to his throngs of expectant and clamoring followers. As the lights dimmed at the altar on the very large stage, I appeared in a grey suit, red tie and white shirt, not a common sight for a black-suited, Roman-collared priest in those days. A team of three lay people, including two women, took turns preaching the Gospel with me, also extraordinary at the time, and hardly common even today.

"Mass of the Future," National Liturgical Conference, Cow Palace, Kansas City, 1967

A Cistercian nun friend from Redwoods Priory in Whitethorn, California, had woven me a large gold and royal blue chasuble for the occasion. When the preaching was completed, I walked over and simply threw the spectacular chasuble over my jacket and tie, and we began the Liturgy of the Eucharist, led by powerful hymns that resonated in the yawning hollows of the Cow Palace.

At Communion time, a large group of male and female Eucharistic ministers spread out in rehearsed order to pass both the bread and the cup through the vast hall, up into the highest balconies. The bread was beautiful loaves of bread-to-be-broken, and not the usual unleavened wafers, and we had gathered several dozen chalices for the wine.

41

It took some time to do all this, of course, but it was somehow a hushed and sacred time. And when the crowd gathered enthusiastically at the end of the service, it was clear that, even if it doesn't sound very avant-garde today, it had been a very special and ground-breaking occasion for liturgical renewal in 1967.

In March of 1967, I was invited to be on an interfaith panel on the "Frontiers of Faith" program on NBC-TV in New York. The dynamic political journalist George Stephanopoulos spoke for the Orthodox tradition, and that was my introduction to Greek Orthodoxy. I also met Rabbi Marc Tanenbaum for the first time there. Marc Tanenbaum was, of course, the father of modern Jewish-Christian dialogue, and it was all a uniquely new ecumenical and interfaith experience.

Woodstock College Relocation

During all this time, my principal residence was at Woodstock College in Maryland, but I was restless to find some new centers for my work and my life, and that kept me on the road a great deal. In January of 1967, I signed a contract with Herder Verlag Freiburg to translate Karl Rahner's *Die Vielen Messen und das Eine Opfer* into English, a project which I later had to abandon in order to work on Woodstock's relocation.

In 1968, I was invited to be a Press Representative at the Fourth Assembly of the World Council of Churches in Uppsala, Sweden, and that was a brief but exciting adventure, milling about with hundreds of interchurch delegates and press people from all around the world.

But my overriding concern became the possible move of Woodstock College into New York. As described earlier, an initial invitation to come to Yale Divinity School in New Haven had been brokered by George Lindbeck in 1965. But that had all been superseded by later discussions with John Bennett and Union Theological Seminary about coming to Morningside Heights in Manhattan, and though negotiations had gone on for some time, that move now had now become a very complex and pressing planning venture.

I continued to be the negotiating agent for Woodstock on the move. In 1968, when discussions finally became detailed and serious, I was living in an apartment at Union. Besides researching places for Woodstock students to live and work in the metropolitan area, I remember exploring one offer to house Woodstock on the fifth floor of the "God Box," the Interchurch Center at 475 Riverside Drive.

I received another offer, from the Dean of the Episcopal Cathedral of St. John the Divine, to house the Woodstock library, which was an object of great envy by many, in the undercroft of the Cathedral, making it an attractive resource not just for theological schools, but for the whole wider community on Morningside Heights. That could have been very imaginative and exciting.

I spent an intriguing morning with the Dean of St. John the Divine and an engineer and an architect, down in the mud of the dark undercroft of the Cathedral, imagining what the library might look like down there.

"Let's put the card catalogue under the high altar over there. How about that?" A great kick for me. And I have thought of the "God Box" just recently, when I read that the National Council of Churches is moving their offices from Morningside Heights to Washington.

To add to the complexity of my mission, 1968 was a turbulent time in the streets of Morningside Heights. An activist named Mark Rudd was leading roaring student demonstrations every day and long into the night, railing against Columbia University for buying up all the property on Morningside Heights.

From my window at Union on 125th Street, I would watch carefully and then go out to join in the demonstrations myself. Power to the People! Then I would quietly move on downtown to the office of Bill Bloor, the Treasurer of Columbia, on Wall Street, to talk about how Woodstock might buy, or negotiate the use of, one or another of Columbia's new acquisitions on Morningside Heights.

My part of all this was a very exciting and complex adventure which did pave the way for Woodstock to move half of its student body from Maryland to Morningside Heights in the fall of 1969. But the college itself closed down a few years later, for many complex reasons.

Woodstock College never formally came to New York, but it later evolved, with its renowned library, into the Woodstock Theological Center at Georgetown University. It still does fine theological and ethical reflection on a whole range of progressive issues.

During these fast-moving and challenging years of

the sixties, I began to lose patience with the political complexity of trying to get a decision out of the many levels of ponderous church bureaucracy that had a say in Woodstock's move—the Cardinal Archbishop of New York, the Jesuit Superiors of the Provinces of Maryland and New York, the Jesuit Curia General and the Vatican hierarchs in Rome.

I would send very detailed reports off to the Vatican and to the General of the Jesuits, and no response would ever come back. A wag once suggested that my reports had just "disappeared behind the Spaghetti Curtain" in Rome.

But the proposed Woodstock move had held the very exciting promise of creating a revolutionary ecumenical and interfaith model of progressive theological education, and I began to feel that I really didn't want to be identified any more with an organization so ecclesiastically muscle-bound that it couldn't seize on such a historic moment.

Lutheran and Episcopal Dialogue Groups

For several years during that time at Woodstock, where I taught the sacramental theology of Eucharist and Orders to Jesuit seminarians, I was a delegate theologian for the U.S. Catholic Bishops in the first national Lutheran-Catholic Conversations and also the first Episcopal-Catholic Conversations, both very exciting fallouts from Vatican II.

Both of these new ecumenical groups were having weekend meetings three times a year in retreat centers around the country, and I had presented a paper with each group on the best of current Catholic sacramental theology, especially on the Eucharist, about which I was wildly enthusiastic.

In the Episcopal-Catholic Dialogue, we came to a consensus as a diverse group of theologians that, with this renewed Roman Catholic understanding of sacramental sign, there was really no disagreement among us as to what is happening at the Lord's Supper, and that it was no longer a controversial issue.

It was a very exciting meeting when both groups of theologians agreed to that doctrinal conclusion, and we decided that at our next meeting, which would be in Mobile, Alabama, we would have a "discrete" intercommunion celebration of the Lord's Supper, and I was asked to create the liturgy for that event.

Whereas usually there would be a Roman Catholic Eucharist on Saturday, at which the Anglicans would stand around, and then an Anglican Eucharist on Sunday, at which the Catholics would stand around, when we met next time in Mobile, we would have a genuine intercommunion celebration, a very first of its kind. There would be no press (and therefore it would be a "discrete" celebration), simply an expression of the theological unity of belief which we in fact all shared about what happens when we gather over the bread and the wine at the Lord's Table.

Each of the national Dialogue Groups consisted of

one or two bishops and five or six theologians from each denomination. So we had asked the bishops on each side to clear what we were going to do in Mobile with higher church offices where necessary.

When I arrived in Mobile for cocktails on Friday evening, my new liturgy in hand, I asked the bishop, Charles Helmsing from Kansas City, what they had said in Rome when he told them what we were going to do the next day. He said, "Oh, I forgot to tell you, but I decided that the time was not right to do this, so we'll have a Catholic Mass tomorrow." No further discussion needed.

During Mass the next morning, celebrated by Bishop Helmsing, I went out for a walk, and when I came into breakfast and was pouring my juice with the others, someone asked where I had been. I quietly replied for all to hear, "I could not be part of what I feel was an unchristian celebration of the Lord's Supper." I wanted to affirm my conviction that the sign value of that Eucharistic action was not representative of the real unity that, as a matter of fact, had consciously and clearly existed between us as we gathered there, and so I could not be part of it.

That was a deeply disturbing personal and theological experience for me. It was the key reason which led me to resign the next day from the national Episcopal-Catholic Dialogue group, and I wrote that I felt the Catholic bishops were interested only in talking unity, but were not committed to taking any concrete action toward actual union of the churches, and I didn't have any more time for that.

It was a very difficult letter for me to write, and when

I wrote the next day from Woodstock also saying the same thing to the bishop in charge of the national Lutheran-Catholic Dialogue Group, he called immediately and asked me to stay on for just one more meeting the next month, with the Lutherans in San Francisco. I had never been to San Francisco, so I agreed.

I was very sensitive to the toxic institutionalism that paralyzed the pre-Vatican II Roman Catholic Church in those days. It is now hard to remember what that was like. I recently came across a letter from Jerome D. Hannan, Bishop of the Diocese of Scranton, to all his priests in 1964. Some of his priests had asked permission to have Scripture Study Groups, or "Bible Services"—hardly revolutionary, I might suggest. In his letter. Bishop Hannan had said:

> In order to assure that Bible Services will not supersede traditional Catholic devotions, especially devotion to the Real Presence of Our Lord in the Blessed Sacrament, I wish to intervene each time when it is proposed to schedule such a Bible Service.
>
> If it is desired to schedule such a service, permission shall be sought from me and, if granted, granted only by me personally.
>
> Moreover, if permission for the Bible Service is granted, it will be on condition that at the beginning of the Service one decade of the Rosary shall be recited with a meditation on the Third Glorious Mystery.

In any case, in February, 1968, when I came to San Francisco for the Lutheran-Catholic Dialogue, I met again with Donna Myers. As a leading lay ecumenist, she was showing one of the more taciturn delegate theologians to the National Lutheran and Catholic Dialogues around San Francisco, and she asked if I would come along to help facilitate the conversation.

I gladly agreed, and we ended our touring with a visit to the Japanese Tea Garden in Golden Gate Park. I have always said that it was there that she dropped the potion in my tea, with a little "kneesies" under the table, and the rest has been living happily ever after. And I would only later realize what a wonderful gift it was for me to have met my future wife on the expense account of the U. S. Catholic Bishops.

I thoroughly enjoyed being involved in those pioneering ecumenical meetings. And I recently read that the Vatican and the Lutheran World Federation have just issued a joint statement, significantly entitled "From Conflict to Communion," saying that there seemed to be no longer any need for these official or high-level Conversations, since most Christians "do not easily see the confessional conflicts of the 16th century as their own conflicts."

I don't know what Martin Luther would have to say about all this, but having been part of all those Conversations for ten years, I can only say "Bravo!

Moving On

In addition to the depressing overload of all this ecclesiastical complexity, it was gradually becoming clear that, at age 39, the way of Roman Catholic celibate priesthood was no longer a growing place for me to be, either as a Christian or as a ministering person.

My vow of celibacy had always been a distinctively creative part of my life, and never a burden beyond my bearing of it. But now I came to recognize that I really needed the love and support of a woman in my life.

It took me the better part of a year to discern the Spirit in this life-changing decision. In the fall of 1968, in addition to living in my apartment at Union in Manhattan, I went to work as a Chaplain for the Medical Mission Sisters in North Philadelphia, and lived in a small cottage on their lovely grounds in Fox Chase. Miriam Therese Winter was a sister of that community, and her wildly popular song "Joy is Like the Rain" was making Fox Chase a thriving center of creative liturgy at that time, in an otherwise deeply conservative Philadelphia Catholicism.

I was delighted to lead that innovative liturgy every day at Fox Chase, often for large numbers of people from the area, and the whole peaceful and contemplative setting left me time to read and think quietly and pray about the decision before me. I shared my internal searchings with several of those wonderful women, and they still remain dear friends to this day.

I recall most especially our very imaginative Christmas Eve liturgy in 1968, with all the children bringing to the altar at the Offertory one of their new stuffed teddy bears or Christmas toys as gifts for poor children. I can still see it in my mind's eye.

I went back to my cottage afterward and remember staying up all of Christmas night wondering whether I really could do without the privilege and joy of leading the Eucharistic community if I moved on. Since my family was nearby, I also had the chance to talk to them about the crucial decision to move on, and that gave me some further support.

In March of 1969, after the Lutheran-Catholic Dialogue in San Francisco where I met Donna Myers for the second time, I finally decided that I would resign my membership in the Jesuit Order and my ecclesiastical priestly ministry. Many priests were doing so in those turbulent post-Vatican II years, and I watched them just shake the dust from their feet and abruptly leave, often in troubled anger. But I wanted to resign my formal ministry and move on from my Jesuit brotherhood in peace and with some style. I remember that to do this with some style was somehow very important to me.

So after a 22-year lifetime of vital Jesuit belonging, and nine of those years as a priest, I wrote to some two hundred fellow Jesuit friends telling them that I intended to move on. Only three responses were negative, and the rest were warm and exceptionally open, mature and respectful of my personal decision, wishing me every blessing.

Working with the Roman Curia was another matter. We had a very dear friend, George Crespin, who was Officialis, or Canon Lawyer, in the Diocese of Oakland. It was through him that I submitted to Rome my petition to resign my ecclesiastical ministry.

The process was to submit a long statement (in Latin, mind you), sketching one's life story and requesting three things: release from the obligations of Celibacy; release from the obligations of Common Life, or living together with other priests; and Reduction to the Lay State. I remember starting off in English, rather than the prescribed Latin, saying that if the Roman officials couldn't understand such a crucial personal document of mine in my native tongue, we really didn't have much to say to one another.

The first two requests, release from my commitment to Celibacy and to Common Life, were to be expected. But, as a professor who was at that time teaching Sacramental Theology and particularly the Sacrament of Orders in a Jesuit seminary, I said that I explicitly did not petition for *"Reduction to the Lay State."*

First of all, I said I resented the implication here that the clerical state of life is superior to, or "higher" than, the lay state, to which one could be "reduced." And further, there is no way that I would now no longer be a priest, but rather *just* a "layman."

When the bishop laid hands on me at my ordination in Innsbruck, he had said, "Thou art a priest forever— *Tu es Sacerdos in Aeternum*—according to the order of Melchisedech." And no amount of distorted canon law or bureaucratic manipulation in curial offices in Rome could ever change that.

As I have so often repeated since then, I am not an ex-priest. I continue to be priest. I am priestly person, as indeed are all baptized Christians. But the whole faith community, in a special way, once laid hands on me with the charism of my sacramental ordination.

In the years that have followed my moving on, it has been a marvelous challenge to exercise and live into that unique call to priestly ministry in lots of other places than those involving traditional ecclesiastical roles. There has been a vital change of persona, it is true. As I have said, I am no longer "Father Tom" as I walk into a room. I am now just Tom, hoping to be as priestly a person as I can be.

Pilgrim Wife On the Journey

In March of 1969, as my decision to resign my ministry was becoming very clear, Donna and I decided to become engaged, and I invited her to come to Philadelphia to meet my family, and to break this news to them. That was a vital and joyful and loving family celebration, and I was vividly aware of my parents' spiritual presence at the table there.

There was a warm and enthusiastic welcome for Donna, although my change of priestly status was a major trauma that some of the family needed time to get used to. In particular, it was exceedingly difficult for us to learn that my sister, Agnes Marie, and her husband,

Stephen, who was a very successful obstetrician, had decided that they could not support my decision to resign my ministry and marry, and that they did not care to come and meet Donna. That very painful and cumbersome distance remained between us and, with great regret, it was never resolved until we had a brief visit with them in 1976.

Donna Myers was born into a Jewish family in St. Paul, Minnesota, in 1929, so we are only a few months apart in age. I have always been grateful that her Jewishness is a grace that has opened me to a special interfaith awareness in my theology and my spirituality in the years since we came together.

Donna's only sibling, Paula, was ten years older, and her father was a pediatrician, plodding with his black bag on house calls through the snows of St. Paul, until he moved his family and his family practice to a warmer clime in Los Angeles in 1941. Political and social consciousness was a prime value in Donna's family, and her first involvement in a Presidential campaign came at the ripe age of seven, when she went knocking on doors for FDR in St. Paul.

At age sixteen, after her junior year in high school in Los Angeles, she went off on the train to the University of Chicago, an intellectual experience from which she says she has never recovered. During her sixth and last year at Robert Hutchins' university in 1951, she was baptized into the Roman Catholic Church. Her sister, Paula, and her brother-in-law, Bud Ogren, were received into the Church in that same year.

After completing her M.A. in Social Studies, Donna worked for the Catholic Labor Alliance in Chicago, and in 1952 she moved to Grailville, the national center of the Grail, located outside Cleveland in Loveland, Ohio. The Grail is an international women's movement—originally Roman Catholic laywomen, but since 1969 explicitly ecumenical, now including Protestant clergy women.

Grail members live in small and informal communities and are all committed to creative spiritual growth and progressive social change. They are not a religious order, but, even dispersed as they are, they have a very special awareness of being vital members of a blessed community.

In 1969, Donna received another M.A., this time in Theology, from the University of San Francisco, just before we married. When we were married, almost half of both our libraries were duplicates and had to be given away. Obviously, it was a match made in heaven.

In April of 1969 I made my break, moved out of my Jesuit house in New York and took a small apartment in Palo Alto, where Donna was an Associate to the Newman Chaplain, John Duryea, in campus ministry at Stanford. I had not received even the courtesy of a reply from the Romans on my request months earlier for dispensation from my ministry commitments, so I decided to move ahead and, pilgrim that I am, the church would just have to catch up with me.

It was a great challenge to begin looking, at age 39, for my first job in the real world. Through our dear friend, Robert McAfee Brown, I learned of an opening to teach in Religious Studies at the University of the Pacific, 90 miles away in Stockton, CA. I breathed a sigh of relief at such a godsend, and not long after was offered the position.

On September 6, 1969, Donna and I were married at First Presbyterian Church in Palo Alto, with Donna's then roommate—and our mutual dear friend—Barbara Troxell, a United Methodist minister, officiating. We had originally planned to be married in the garden of the Newman Center Chapel, and we had invited people to come there.

But three days before the date, a *Palo Alto Times* reporter wanted breathlessly to headline that this Newman Associate was about to marry an ex-priest at the Newman Center. Fearing that John Duryea could well be sacked for permitting us to marry at the Newman Center, we quietly moved the wedding down the street to First Presbyterian Church and just waved along our arriving guests in time for the ceremony.

To add to that drama, the day before the wedding I came down with a pair of very painful kidney stones. I can still remember Donna coming with her dear mother to my bedside in Stanford Hospital, and both of them saying: "You're going to get married tomorrow anyway, so you might as well get up!" Which of course I did, and the kidney stones passed, just in time.

Along with many members of the Myers clan from all over California, we were delighted that my brother, Charlie, and his wife, Ann, came from Philadelphia to celebrate with us. It was a glorious sunny day, and we had

Tom and Donna with Barbara Troxell at their wedding in Palo Alto, 1969

our reception on the lawn of the Newman Center, with family members and throngs of well-wishers all around us.

Then, after a five day honeymoon in Carmel, almost torpedoed by a disastrous blowout on the highway down, I became an Associate Professor in Religious Studies at the University of the Pacific in 1969. I was the first non-Methodist to teach Religous Studies in this small and lively United Methodist school, and Donna and I moved to Stockton right away. We bought a fine little house close to campus and found ourselves comfortable and warmly challenged in a bright new city for the next eight years.

My undergraduate theology courses for the next eight years at UOP were interdisciplinary with literature and the applied social sciences, and I thoroughly enjoyed the excitement of team teaching with other faculty. I was promoted to Professor with Tenure in 1972, and then finally resigned in good standing in 1977.

Israel, Palestine, and the Middle East

A wonderful part of the University of the Pacific program was its Winter Term, where students did only one course in the month of January, meant to be an innovative, project-oriented kind of research. In 1971, I offered a travel seminar to Israel, entitled *"Jewish-Christian Dialogue: The Search for Religious Identity."* My Christian students would explore their own religious identity by asking what it means to be a Jew in Israel.

So Donna and I took ten students to Israel for three weeks. It was the first of our several trips to Israel, and it was a marvelous experience. We had a superb guide with us for the whole time, a series of seminars set up for us by the Jewish Agency in Jerusalem on all facets of Israeli life, and the opportunity to see rather well, even if briefly, a good part of the whole country.

I challenged my undergraduates to go out and meet lots of Israeli Jews and to probe with them their own religious identity as Christians, and I recalled the words of

Bonhoeffer: "Only the one who cries out for the Jews has a right to sing Gregorian Chant."

We were troubled by the continuing conflict between Arabs and Jews, and the ever-present tension one felt in the air. We were deeply moved by the fragility of the refugee camps we visited, the understandable reactions we encountered in the Arabs we met in the Old City of Jerusalem, and the seeming impossibility of a peaceful settlement of so many very human problems.

All of this fed my growing interest in the complexities of life in that painful part of the world. And, for the first time, I began to wonder who would ever speak up for the Palestinians, and that later became an obsession of mine.

Then, catching my breath just a bit, I served in 1972-73 as Assistant Director of the Western Regional Office of the American Association of University Professors, on leave from UOP and living in Palo Alto. I responded to complaints in thirteen western states on the governance of colleges and universities, academic freedom and tenure, due process and collective bargaining. It was very satisfying to travel widely and to often be personally instrumental in the resolution of academic conflict and the implementation of sound principles of professional conduct.

While at the University of the Pacific, I got caught up in drafting faculty grievance and dismissal hearing procedures for the University, and chairing the first faculty committee ever convened there to hear charges for dismissal brought against a tenured faculty member, whom I knew and admired. Challenging, and painful.

Such formal procedures were brand new at most universities at that time. My AAUP experience proved to be very valuable, and I continue to have great respect for the remarkable effectiveness of AAUP principles in the academic world. Colleges and universities would be very different places without it.

In the fall of 1973, Donna and I went back to Israel for a sabbatical, this time without students so that I could concentrate on research at the International Institute for Advanced Theological Studies in Tantur, on the road between Jerusalem and Bethlehem. But we decided to get some taste for Arab life and culture before this four-month stay in Israel.

So we spent nearly a month—ten days in Lebanon, four days in Jordan, and twelve days in Egypt—before heading back to the Institute in Tantur. In each country we had good contacts who were wonderfully helpful in sending us on to others. They all led us through a powerful political, cultural and theological education, and it deeply affected our Israeli experience.

Beirut is a very sophisticated city, a good introduction to the Middle East—Oriental, yes, but still very Western as well. The airport was a confusion of noisy crowds, military frisks and customs inspectors, and we had not a clue as to the Arabic language spoken or written all around us. I remember how terribly frustrating that was for an old linguist like me.

The mood was not as tense as we had expected, but military checkpoints were everywhere and rumors of a coming showdown with the Palestinians reminded

us that the calm was still very tenuous. Most of the
Lebanese we met had strongly non-political views. They
just wanted peace so they could get on with their own
social development, prosperity and thriving tourism.
Palestinians were their brothers, yes, but their presence in
Lebanon meant a lot of trouble.

Of all the Arab countries, Lebanon has by far the
largest proportion of Christians to Muslims, almost 50%
of the total population. When we asked several Maronite
Christians if they thought of themselves as Arabs, they
said "No, we're Phoenicians!" So, to our old question
"What is a Jew?" an equally complex one was now added,
"What is an Arab?"

We drove to every corner of the country, deeply
moved by the beauty and awe of such places as Byblos
and Baalbeck, both ancient Phoenician cities with spectacular ruins, and finally to the more familiar Biblical
cities of Tyre and Sidon.

We visited overnight in Tyre, which is almost on the
Israeli border and a heavily Muslim area. We met with
the Lebanese director of excavations there, Pierre Bikai,
and his archeologist wife, Patricia, who was a doctoral
candidate at the Graduate Theological Union in Berkeley
and the sister of a friend of ours from Stockton, Elaina
Coyne.

We had a first-class tour of the famous dig and a
painful discussion of Israeli commando raids in the area,
which gave us another viewpoint indeed. We slept glori-
ously open under the stars on their roof, overlooking
the sea and the ruins of the ancient city. All went well

until the Muslim call to prayer from the minarets of two nearby mosques roused us—the first at 4 AM, for twenty minutes, and the next at 4:30 AM. The sunrise was breathtaking over the necropolis!

Our final dinner in Beirut was a full Lebanese mezze with a family whose relatives in Palo Alto had sent us to them. It was about forty dishes in all, with arak (or anis) to drink and a bubbly water pipe to smoke along the way. "I can't believe I ate all that!" and "Try it, you'll like it!"

We then moved on to Jordan. In Amman, the capital city, we stayed in the Hotel Philadelphia, which was originally the name of Amman in ancient times. Although the largest city in Jordan, Amman is a rather small and unsophisticated town, compared to Beirut. We had a rather fascinating visit to Jerash, a well-preserved Roman town in a quiet valley to the north, among the Biblical mountains of Gilead, and then on to Madaba, The City of Mosaics, where underneath almost every house lies a fine Byzantine mosaic. The radiant pastel coloring of it all is dazzling.

But our greatest adventure was a very long day's trip to Petra, which is an ancient and fabled Nabatean city carved right into the rose-red sandstone cliffs, 150 miles into the desert south of Amman. The final entrance into Petra, The Lost City of Stone, is a half-hour guided ride on horseback through a very narrow canyon gorge, and then the awesome carved redstone city suddenly opens up to you. It was a day long to remember.

We will never forget our visits to three refugee camps, two with Deborah Schak, who represented the

Pontifical Mission for Palestine in Jordan, and one with Joe Thompson, who directed refugee work for the Lutheran World Federation. In all the camps, we were deeply moved by the terrible poverty and the overcrowding, and by one-room tin shacks for a whole family, with mud and flies and open sewers everywhere.

About 70,000 Palestinian refugees lived in Baaka, the largest camp in Jordan. It was built for displaced persons after the 1967 war, some of whom were already refugees from Israel in 1948 and then displaced again from the West Bank in 1967. We felt almost like voyeurs going into their hovels; it's not easy to look unashamedly into the eyes of such human misery. I began to understand why, after growing up for twenty-five years in these camps, a young Palestinian turns to the guerillas.

Among other conversations, we had a most enlightening morning with Bishop Naaman Simaan, Roman Catholic Bishop for East Jordan. He was very pro-Palestinian, with intelligent and articulate observations. He was convinced that Zionism is an expansionist threat to all land "from the Euphrates to the Nile." This was the first time we had heard that phrase, and we often heard it from Arabs, especially later in Egypt.

As we moved on for our twelve days in Egypt, Cairo was a whole new scene: a city of five million, extremely hot and humid, just teeming with people all day and night, and with miserable poverty far more evident than in Lebanon or Jordan. We spent almost a full day in the Egyptian Antiquities Museum, a fantastic collection that thrilled us.

We took our time visiting the awesome Egyptian pyramids and the Great Sphinx of Giza, once by moonlight and then again in the morning sun. We took a five-day trip on a creaky old train, a Hungarian reject that the Russians had pawned off on Nasser. We went about 500 miles up the Nile (really south!), first to Luxor, site of the ancient city of Thebes and known as "the world's greatest open air museum," and then on to the awesome Aswan High Dam.

The tombs of the Pharaohs (including Tutankamun, "King Tut") across the Nile in the Valley of the three Kings were especially marvelous. But the magnificent Temple Complex of Karnak, a vast ancient Egyptian temple precinct, really took our breath away with its colorful and awesome beauty.

Karnak is an enormous mix of decayed temples, chapels, and colored pylons built over 2,000 years before Christ. The complex sprawls magnificently on the east bank of the Nile in ancient Thebes, which is modern-day Luxor. It is a derelict place, but it is said to be still capable of overshadowing many of the wonders of the modern world. In its day, its colossal main temple must have been awe-inspiring. It certainly is breathtaking even today.

Almost the only inhabitable land in the vast country of Egypt is in the narrow green belt along the Nile. In 1973, there were 35 million people jammed into it, no doubt many more today. The Aswan High Dam is awesome in size and brilliant beauty, and the huge Lake Nasser created by it has been a tremendous boon for development, especially in the very backward villages of Upper Egypt.

Simone Tagher, an Egyptian at that time the International President of the Grail Movement and living in Cairo, was very helpful in putting us together with all the people we met in Egypt. In addition to a number of evening groups which she arranged, we also had a long morning with Bishop Samuel, the Coptic Orthodox Bishop of Cairo "for Public, Ecumenical and Social Services."

I can still hear him quietly say, "Israel is every bit as racist as South Africa," and then develop that thesis at some length. Interestingly, a South African Jewish immigrant couple whom we later met in Haifa agreed with him. It was still another viewpoint to digest.

Bishop Samuel was a remarkable man, and I later followed his career. In 1981, he was killed by a grenade while representing his faith in an ecumenical celebration in Cairo. He was sitting in a reviewing stand with Egyptian President Anwar Sadat, watching a military parade, and he was killed in the same assassin's grenade attack which killed the President.

So, after our wonderful time in Lebanon, Jordan and Egypt, we went back again to Israel, for my four months as one of thirty international resident scholars in the beautiful marble buildings of the Ecumenical Institute at Tantur. It was a striking complex of shining buildings newly built on a hill overlooking Jerusalem and Bethlehem, with the royal mountains of Moab, twenty miles away across the Jordan, visible on a clear day.

Our community of several dozen scholars was drawn from twenty countries, communicating in English and French, and representing all shades of the Protestant, Catholic and Eastern Orthodox traditions. We had a remarkable range of worship services, and wonderful discussions on all sorts of interfaith issues.

I brought with me to Tantur in 1973 all the reading materials I had gathered on Liberation Theology, which at that time was an exciting new movement, and I wanted to see what it had to say about what was happening in Israel. On Yom Kippur, when we left the dining room for a siesta, the whole country was quiet because it is forbidden by Jewish law to turn a switch of any kind on this most sacred of holy days.

Just as we were dropping off to sleep, we were awakened by sirens and we turned on the radio to hear only a somber list of regiment numbers calling up the Israeli Defense Forces to active duty. This was their first military action since the Six Day War in 1967, six years earlier. For several days the government issued no statistics at all on killed or wounded in the severe fighting in the Sinai and on the Golan Heights. We kept our heads down together, nervously straining to look for Egyptian planes from our rooftop.

Donna and I drafted a statement for the international group of scholars at Tantur on the collision of rights of both the Israelis and the Palestinians, to be published in the *Jerusalem Post*, and we posted it on the bulletin board outside the dining room. The next morning we found a swastika scrawled on the letter, indicating that the staff of the house, who were all West Bank Arabs, did not appreciate our statement.

There really was no place to hide, no room for "objective" observers. Blood was spilling on the sand—as it still is today—and I still struggle with the challenge of how to be a reconciling force in a conflict of rights that seem so irreconcilable.

While we were at Tantur, we were somehow too distracted by the threat of Egyptian air raids to ever directly face the issue of Palestine. It is interesting, as I reflect on it, that in all that time I rarely talked at any length to a Palestinian. We were several times briefly in the homes of educated Palestinians, sent by our Stockton friends, Tasha and David Stadtner. But, for the most part, the political issue of Palestine was rarely seriously considered.

In all its complexity, that experience of being a resident scholar on the road between Jerusalem and Bethlehem has colored all my later work and my passions on Israeli-Palestinian issues. While there, I wrote an article, "Dialogue in Jerusalem: Christian Support for Israel?" which was published in the *Journal of Ecumenical Studies*, and I have no more answers today than I had then.

Perhaps our real "peak experience" of that time in the Middle East was climbing to the top of Mount Sinai at 1.30 AM on the last day of the year, a fantastically grand and awesome occasion. From the peak of the great Mount Sinai both Israeli and Arab territory is visible, and it seemed somehow a fitting Biblical way to end our stay in that land which is at once so holy and unholy, so earthy in its passions and yet so mysteriously transcendent.

But let me jump ahead for a bit. About sixteen years later, on the day after Christmas in 1989, all of this experience had a very moving sequel. While living in San Francisco, I got a call from a Palestinian group inviting me to spend ten days travelling and listening in the West Bank and Gaza. All expenses would be paid, they said, and I would only speak to Palestinians across the Green Line, not in Israel itself.

We would be a delegation of six people, half of whom would be Palestinian-Americans. When I asked what would be expected of me when I returned, I was told I could do whatever I wished with what I saw. I simply had to be at the San Francisco airport by midnight that night if I wished to go. I agreed, and it was one of the most disturbing experiences of my life.

Donna and I had, of course, lived for extended periods in Israel and on the West Bank before, and we had travelled to the Gaza Strip and through many West Bank towns and villages, but I was not ready for the experience of seeing the State of Israel through Palestinian eyes. As is probably still the case today, the climate of violence was almost beyond belief, and the hopes for a peaceful settlement between Palestinian and Jew seemed to recede a bit more into tears every day.

On that visit, I remember once going into the rocky rubble of a former Palestinian home in the early evening. In the dusky remains of what had been the basement of his house, we saw a very old bearded Palestinian man in tears, huddled around a fire to keep himself warm.

We sat down with him and asked him what had

happened. He said there had been a knock on his door and an Israeli trooper wanted to know where his son was, presumably on suspicion that his son was a Palestinian activist of some kind. He replied that he didn't know where his son was, and that was the truth. So the Israelis bulldozed his house on the spot in the dead of night, and he was sitting there telling us his story. I can still see him in my mind's eye as I recall that profound experience. Such violence and brutality is not a unique experience for many Palestinians, but rarely does one ever hear about it.

In the months following my return in 1991, I worked with a group in San Francisco trying to bring together a Christian-Jewish-Muslim Task Force on the Middle East, but events in the Arabian Peninsula complicated those efforts almost to a standstill. However, since that brief but very intense experience of being only with Palestinians, I have been immersed in everything that is happening on all sides in the West Bank and Gaza. I keep up with almost daily events and have a file about eight inches thick. The ongoing injustice of the Israeli occupation of the "Palestinian territories" simply infuriates me.

It is absolutely clear that UN Resolutions 242 and 338 make it internationally illegal for the Israelis to occupy and continue to hold the Palestinian territory which they took over in the 1967 war. That all began now more than forty years ago, and my own country's blind and shameful support for that injustice allows it to continue without any serious question. The eyes of the whole world have just turned away.

In San Francisco, 1977

U.S. financial support for the state of Israel has been an astronomical $117 billion in the last forty years, with no accountability whatsoever, and with almost no awareness of that fact by the American people. Reliable reports indicate that Israel is now receiving $3.1 billion every year, all of it in military aid. Negotiations are underway to raise that to $3.6 billion in 2013. In a time of expanding needs in this country, that is a huge amount of money. And key to it all is that 75% of this military aid must be spent with U.S. military contractors, and that makes Israel a very large customer of those contractors.

All of this explains the almost insuperable power of the Israel lobby in Washington, and it also means that every square foot of Palestinian territory illegally occupied by Israeli troopers and settlers in the last forty years has been bought and paid for by U.S. taxpayers As one of those taxpayers, I take that very seriously, and the injustice of it all saddens and pains me deeply.

In 2013, the United Nations has at last declared that the Palestinian "territories" are no longer just territories, but are now the formally recognized State of Palestine, and that Israeli occupation of those territories is in fact the internationally illegal invasion of a sovereign nation. But I suspect it will be a long time before that crucial distinction will ever be well enough known, or even cared about, to make any real political difference for Palestinians in their call for justice.

I have had several invitations to return to Israel since 1990, but I have never returned. I find that I simply could not abide being in the presence of an Israeli Defense Force trooper, and I grope for some way to come to grips with that deeply disturbing feeling. How to be a peace maker in all this is just an extraordinary challenge, and very painful.

I often share the terrible pain of it all with our very dear Palestinian Christian friends here at Pilgrim Place, Rizek and Alice Abusharr. Their ancestors in Jerusalem go back 500 years, and Rizek was for 51 years on the staff of the YMCA in West Jerusalem, retiring as the longtime Director General. They are American citizens, and he is an internationally respected spokesperson for Palestinian rights. I can barely imagine what it must mean for the Abusharrs to see what their own country, and mine, is now doing to their Palestinian people.

My Wife the Lawyer

When we came home from our four months in Tantur in 1973, Donna started preparing to go off for her three years at Stanford Law School. As she was applying there, she one night murmured at dinner that she wasn't really sure about going to law school, since, as she said, "I'm going to be 48 before I'm an attorney." Taking a deep breath, I replied that she would be 48 anyway, so she might as well be 48 and an attorney. That wise pastoral word seemed to do it, and the rest is history. Oh, that Jesuit training!

While Donna was a law student, we both became active members of First Presbyterian Church in Palo Alto. I was ordained a Ruling Elder there and served for three years on the Session. As I took on those commitments, the congregation accepted our theological conviction that it did not make sense for us to "become" Presbyterians, that we came to membership and service in that congregation as "transdenominational Christians with roots in the Roman Catholic tradition," and I have so described myself ever since. Sometimes my gay and lesbian friends ask: "You're a "trans-what?— but I still find it the most theologically accurate way I have to describe myself.

In spring of 1975, again with the help of Robert McAfee Brown, I set up a "Research Project on Innovative Theological Learning," administering two planning grants of $55,000 each from the Eli Lilly Endowment. Bob Brown and I had been dreaming of what might someday become a national center to translate Third

World Liberation Theology onto the North American scene, to explore interdisciplinary models of contextual learning that would relate theological values to the applied social sciences.

We were both thinking big, and I was breathless at the possibilities. These models are commonplace and even old hat today, but I thrill to remember what an exciting and brand new vision it all was in those days.

I did my organizing work on the Lilly project while living with Donna in Stanford student housing in Palo Alto, and I commuted several days a week for two semesters to teach at University of the Pacific in Stockton. I believe that the Lilly work was a really significant project that opened lots of new vistas at that time. It took me to parishes and universities interested in social justice issues all through San Francisco and the Bay Area, and I enjoyed it immensely.

In June, 1977, Donna graduated from Stanford Law School. Neither of us was ever much into the pomp and circumstance of such occasions, but we played the whole script this time, in a giddy ritualizing of relief over three hard years behind us. After all, she was now 48 and she was almost an attorney! She still had to pass the Bar exam to be an attorney, but she could say that she was a "J.D." It was a splendid occasion with throngs of family and friends cheering in the quadrangle, and with only a few grey hairs under the gold-tasseled cap of the sweet young graduate this time.

The Grand Recessional had hardly faded when it was time to begin cramming for the Bar Exam. I felt like an

Olympic Games Trainer for the next seven weeks, but the hurdle of the three-day Bar Exam was finally over at the end of July and we collapsed for a few weeks of vacation in the Sierras.

In September, 1977, Donna accepted a position with the National Labor Relations Board in San Francisco. I had recently resigned my tenured teaching position at the University of the Pacific, and we sold our house in Stockton and moved to San Francisco.

We bought a wonderful bright apartment on the top floor of a three-story co-op complex on Ellis Street, right in the shadow of the magnificent St. Mary's Cathedral and just next door to our dear friend, Barbara Troxell. It had lots of stained redwood, a grand front porch and huge bay windows looking out over the Cathedral and south over the whole city, and I thrived on hiking the blue green hills in the morning sunshine.

That co-op apartment on Ellis Street remains the most wonderful place we have ever lived in. When we decided to move to Pilgrim Place in Claremont, we were dismayed that we had to sell it because, as a co-op, it had to be owner-occupied. So we've been terribly sorry never to have had it for later visits to the city—or now even for use by our Pilgrim Place friends.

Donna began doing good legal work for the National Labor Relations Board. Not long after, two other passage points occurred. The first was the death of Donna's mother, Norma Myers, on November 30, 1977, not long after having proudly seen her daughter graduate from Stanford Law School. Norma was a great human being, known to all of her adoring children and grandchildren as "Goomie."

She was a real "valiant woman," with a splendidly full and happy history of 82 years behind her. She was only sick for three weeks, and her death was a good and peaceful one, in her own bed. We celebrated all of that in a marvelous liturgy of thanksgiving, with 175 family and friends gathered in a family back yard in Los Angeles. She continues to be sorely missed.

Then, as we arrived back in San Francisco the next day, Donna got word that she had passed the Bar Exam and would be formally admitted to the California Bar on December 21. After four months of waiting, the news brought great relief, and it made for the best Christmas we ever had.

Having resigned my position at UOP, I set out to become an independent "career guidance specialist." I began to find the field of career development very adaptable to the issues I wanted to raise with people in a theological perspective.

In my search for problems that are real issues for large numbers of people, around which theological reflection might be centered, the whole area of work became more and more central. Across racial and gender and class lines, work is a core concern for just about everyone, from young students through the middle-aged unemployed, and even to the elders all around us here at Pilgrim Place. Donna's work on labor issues has always complemented all of this for me, and I've appreciated that immensely.

50th birthday celebration, rafting on the Colorado River, 1980

Before long, I heard of two women who had similar interests to mine in the work world, and in 1978 I joined forces with a very talented friend from Stockton days, Kathy Mondragon, and with Marna McKenzie, a Presbyterian minister who was in campus ministry at San Francisco State University. With their help, I designed a distinctive Career/Life Planning process and led three-day workshops in what we called "Work-Net," working in parishes and colleges all over northern California to develop a mind-set for changing careers easily.

Work-Net was an exciting process of consciousness-raising and empowerment, developing a practical strategy for job hunting and creative work alternatives. I still remain deeply committed to helping people find, and even create for themselves, careers that draw on their very best talents and passions and values.

In all my teaching of undergraduates, and also in all

my pastoral work of so many kinds, this vision has always remained central. Employment, or what I call "good work," is the central area where personal empowerment can become possible, and it has always been a major focus for me in all the counseling I ever do.

At the University of San Francisco, I taught a course on Career Planning for undergraduates who were doing an internship with business and industry for a semester, and also a Social Ethics and Career Development course in Continuing Education, where we worked a lot on work and personal empowerment. I also taught similar courses at the Jesuit School of Theology in Berkeley, as well as at churches in Seattle and Albuquerque and back East in Bridgeport, Connecticut and Richmond, Virginia.

The Social Justice Commission

Then came one of my most challenging adventures. I remember the day in 1980 when I first got the idea of going to work for the Archdiocese of San Francisco. There was an opening for Executive Director of the Commission on Social Justice, and I went to see the person who was leading the social justice work in the archdiocese, a great priest named Cuchulain Moriarty.

When I asked him where he ever got such a wonderful name, he said that his father was an Irish poet and "he once told me that he named me Cuchulain because Cuchulain means 'compassionate warrior' in Gaelic, and he wanted his son to be a compassionate warrior." It took a little selling, but the Compassionate Warrior convinced

Archbishop John Quinn that he should hire this renegade priest as his new Social Justice Director, and I was appointed on July 1, 1980. A wonderful four years lay ahead of me.

I was at first hesitant to be invited back into the church and clerical network, but it turned out to be remarkably pleasant. To my surprise, I was very well received by fellow priests and I was given major responsibility in the Archdiocese for interpreting Catholic social teaching as it applies to issues of structural injustice. The staff was expanded from two to six persons and the budget from $30,000 to $140,000. We later raised $250,000 from foundation and other sources.

Then I began my deep commitments to Central America, as well as to trade unions, and these have both lasted for many years. I travelled several times to the refugee camps in El Salvador and Guatemala and got involved with American human rights groups working there against the terrible destructive influence of the United States in supporting the Contras in Central America.

One of my most exciting ventures at the Commission was a coalition I put together in 1981 with the longshoremen in the San Francisco Labor Council. Herb Mills, the Secretary of Local 10 of the International Longshore and Warehouse Union, the ILWU, called me one day. Herb was one of the most remarkable characters I had ever met. He had a Ph.D. in Social Sciences from UC Berkeley and was a brawny stevedore with a blistering vocabulary that just demanded attention.

Hearing of my interest in justice and Central America, Herb told me that the longshoremen wanted to boycott sending any military cargo to El Salvador. He said they couldn't do it by themselves and that they needed support from the churches. I agreed to help, and we got statements of support from two Catholic bishops and eight heads of Protestant churches, as well as from many local congregations.

The ILWU decision was announced at a joint union-church press conference just before Christmas and then celebrated wildly in the cavernous Union Hall on the waterfront. We had many church representatives there, and it was a roaring statement of solidarity which I still remember.

The longshoremen refused to load any military cargo bound for El Salvador, not just in San Francisco but all up and down the West Coast. The prospects for a whole new coalition of labor and the religious community were very promising, and we later began to work together against Ku Klux Klan violence toward Blacks in the Bay Area. That was all a great experience.

In early 1982, we got deeply involved in bringing the churches into the Nuclear Freeze Movement and I served on the Executive Committee for Proposition 12, Californians for a Bilateral Nuclear Weapons Freeze. One day I got a phone call from Harold Willens, a very wealthy Jewish radical in Los Angeles. He asked me if I could get Archbishop Quinn to endorse the Nuclear Freeze and I said I would try.

So for the feast day of St. Francis on October 4, in the

city of San Francisco, I wrote a speech for the Archbishop in which he gave his enthusiastic support for the Nuclear Freeze Campaign. We had splendid network billing, and a *New York Times* article even talked about the Catholic Church joining the ranks of the "peace churches."

In June, Donna and I had a wonderful three weeks in Europe, and it was a welcome break. I had been invited to represent the National Conference of Catholic Bishops at a German-American consultation on nuclear disarmament at Bad Boll, near Stuttgart. After that meeting, we travelled down to Innsbruck, Salzburg and Vienna, visiting a lot of my old haunts from Jesuit student days, and then on to Budapest.

We had some good contacts in Hungary, and had several wonderful meals with families there. I can still see us warmly sitting with them around their dinner tables. It was a fascinating experience, and I would go back to Eastern Europe anytime.

Meanwhile, more than a hundred parishes of the archdiocese were working on the Nuclear Freeze, and the Commission joined an Initiative for the ballot in November of 1982, calling for a bilateral freeze with the Soviet Union on the production and deployment of nuclear weapons.

To support that Initiative and continue our work on the nuclear issue, we formally set up the Nuclear Disarmament Project, a Paulo Freire-based education/action program on nuclear issues in parishes and schools in three Bay Area counties. Pia Moriarty, who knew a great deal about Paulo Freire, was a superb organizer in the parishes, and that wonderful project did very good work.

Dianne Feinstein was Mayor of San Francisco while I was at the Commission. She appointed me to the City's Human Relations Commission in 1982. She asked me to help with her campaign to buy back all the handguns in the City and County of San Francisco. Police believed that there were about 800,000 handguns in our city of 700,000 people—one under each pillow, one by the front and back door, one in the glove compartment, although no one knew who had a gun.

The Mayor wanted to buy back enough guns to melt them down and make a statue of Saint Francis. Although she never got enough for the statue, we collected lots of guns in the city and in all the parishes. I was very proud of the project, and felt that it had been good work. I recently was happy to see that Dianne Feinstein is still working on the issue of handgun control even today.

Swearing-in at the San Francisco Human Relations Commission, City Hall, 1982

Ricardo Calderon

One of the great events of my time at the Commission came in the fall of 1983 when I led a delegation to San Salvador to work for the release of a political prisoner, Ricardo Calderon. I think it was the most difficult and challenging experience of my life.

Our office had been deeply involved with El Salvador and Guatemala, and with their refugees who were pouring into the Bay Area all the time. One night we had a meeting with Elliott Abrams, Assistant Secretary of State, who had called to ask for the meeting to "find out what church people were thinking" about the Reagan policy on human rights in Central America. I was delighted to oblige.

We gathered a large interfaith group, the core of our activist network, and told him rather forcefully what we thought for three hours. With a roving microphone, we really laid into Abrams, especially since he had asked for what we thought of the Reagan support for the Contras. He might still remember that meeting. But U.S. arms continued to flow to Central America and our country stubbornly remained on the wrong side. And for our part, we continued to protest the shame of it all.

Ricardo Calderon was Secretary General of the University of El Salvador. He had been kidnapped and tortured, and was being held without charges with 415 other political detainees in Mariona Prison in San Salvador. Through Amnesty International and various U.S. faculty groups, a national campaign of letters to

Ambassador Thomas Pickering and Salvadoran President Alvaro Magaña had been mounted, demanding Calderon's release on human rights grounds.

After five days of very tense discussions, the time seemed right to apply the final pressure to get him out, and we succeeded. His case had captured the attention of many outside El Salvador, including many Americans in the Bay Area and far beyond, and they began a "Free Calderon" movement to support us. While we were there, a contingent of reporters from CBS News and the *Washington Post* was covering our every move.

Besides myself, representing the Archbishop and the Commission, our delegation to get Calderon's release included a medical doctor, an immigration attorney who is now a Senator in the California Legislature, Bill Monning, and Bill Kraus, a staffer for Representative Sala Burton, whose office was very helpful with moving us through our diplomatic maze. After meeting with the Ambassador and other staff of the American Embassy, we met for ninety minutes with President Magaña in his office and negotiated his commitment to release Calderon.

But it took us another eleven long days of tense back-and-forth and waiting before we finally got him. During that time, some thirty members of Congress made calls or sent cables to Pickering and Magaña, as did literally thousands of other folks from around the country. We were very conscious of speaking in the name of this vast national network of concerned people, and that realization was a great support for us.

Returning with Ricardo Calderon, San Francisco Airport, November, 1983

We met with Ricardo in Mariona prison four times. On the eleventh day, we were convinced that we had failed, and we went in exhausted depression to tell him that we were going home the next day. Then, at 5:05 PM, the Director of the prison came into the room where we were and handed Ricardo his letter of release.

It was unbridled but still muted exhilaration. Magaña and Pickering told us that people in town knew that we were there, and that it was dangerous for us to travel without an armored car for protection. So the embassy provided that for us, and, with Calderon crouched down on the floor, we raced off to the airport.

Still under heavy guard even in the plane, we flew out with Ricardo, his wife, his mother-in-law, and his gorgeous infant son, Papi, all safe and sound. When we arrived at two o'clock the next morning in the San

Francisco airport, we were greeted by a jubilant crowd of press and "Free Calderon" activists who had been following our every move. I shall never forget what an intensely emotional moment that was.

It took some months for me to digest the whole Calderon experience, but some things had become clearer than ever. What must it have been like for Salvadorans to live under such outrageous terror all the time? It was obvious to me, and to anyone who really cared, that the revolutionary forces were winning in El Salvador. The right-wing death squads, the Contras, were clearly out of control and were terrorizing the entire country.

During the twelve days we were there, twenty-six brutally mutilated bodies had been found on the streets and garbage dumps of San Salvador alone, and I remember seeing gruesome pictures of them every morning in all the papers.

Everyone knew who the leaders of the death squads were, but the Pentagon generals and the Reagan ideologues refused to use their power to force the Salvadoran government to arrest them. With mounting public pressure for military intervention by the United States, I worked with Archbishop Quinn on a pastoral letter which he issued in October of 1983, calling for a radical change of policy on Central America, and for us to stop committing fighting troops "where we have no right to be."

I was glad that we were not all alone on this. John Quinn's pastoral letter repeated a strong critical position which the National Conference of Catholic Bishops had recently taken on the U.S. Central American policy, and that was all very valuable in the organizing which the Commission on Social Justice was doing in the religious community on this critically dangerous situation.

In all of this work, along with Cuchulain, two dynamo women back home, Martha Wood and Pia Moriarty, warmly supported me and kept the Commission going. I have already mentioned how Pia, remarkable organizer that she was, had inspired and led all of our fantastic work in the parishes on the Nuclear Freeze Campaign. We have known Pia since her Stanford student years, and she did a splendid job in designing our wedding invitations during a summer at Grailville. She and her musician husband, Bob Hurd, have now happily joined us as Pilgrim Place residents, and that gives us both great pleasure.

The Commission on Social Justice gave me a remarkable platform for four years to speak out on justice issues, more so than in any of my previous incarnations, and much of that credibility derived from the progressive political and social position which the church was beginning to represent, thanks in no small part to the heroic example of the Salvadoran people.

Early on at the Commission, we had set up legislative advocacy programs at local, state and congressional levels, with extensive media coverage on what we were doing. As word got out on all that, I was invited in 1981 to host my own Sunday morning program called "Mosaic" on KPIX Channel 5, the local CBS affiliate in San Francisco. It was rather early in the morning and not exactly prime time, but I could choose whomever I

wanted to interview on social and political issues for a
half-hour, and that for twenty-six weeks in each of the
next two years.

The program was aired again after the late night
movie, when, to my great astonishment, the station said
there were up to 200,000 viewers. I couldn't believe there
were that many insomniacs interested in social justice!
It was a wide-ranging and challenging time, involving me
with lots of interesting and well-known people, and the
phone calls I triggered on the program kept us going on
lots of new concerns. My TV interviews easily became
my own Sunday worship service.

The End of the Affair

In 1984, one of my most effective calls for action
came back to haunt me, and it brought my career at the
Commission on Social Justice to a crashing halt. Way
back in 1981, when I was just new at the job and only
beginning on Sunday morning TV, I had received a
phone call from a viewer saying, "Mr. Social Justice, what
are you going to do about all these kids who are coming
out of Catholic dance halls on Saturday nights to beat up
on gay and lesbian people in the Castro District?"

In response, we created a fifteen-person Task Force
on Gay and Lesbian Issues, chaired by theologian and
psychotherapist Kevin Gordon. We resolved to develop
a city-wide educational program "against violent acts to
anyone, regardless of their life-style," and to constructive-
ly implement the 1976 Declaration of the United States

Bishops which, quite remarkably for such an early time, had declared:

> Homosexuals, like everyone else, should not suffer from prejudice against their basic human rights. They have a right to respect, friendship, and justice. They should have an active role in the Christian community.

The Task Force worked for several months and produced a 120-page report with 54 strong recommendations. It was endorsed by the American Psychological Association and warmly received by the gay and lesbian community far and wide. 10,000 copies were sold around the world, and it also got some space in *Time* and *Newsweek*.

Our challenging work on gay and lesbian issues had already created rumblings all around us for several years. And now, with such new publicity, I knew that this report would deeply upset lots of people in the clergy, including my own boss, Archbishop Quinn.

Finally, in Holy Week, 1984, a nervous and very formal Monsignor came to my office door from "the Arch" to say that I was to be replaced by "someone more conservative," and that I should pack up and be out of my office by morning. As I had feared, the Report on Gay and Lesbian Issues had finally been the last straw.

A large and very angry crowd met in our living room that night to organize a protest of the firing, but I said that I had only so much political capital to spend, and I would spend it where I thought it most valuable, so we'll just move on from here.

My getting unceremoniously sacked was a very painful and bruising time, redeemed only by the warm and vocal support of a wonderful wide community of friends and colleagues from years of coalition-building on social justice issues. I negotiated six months severance pay from the Archdiocese; and when the dust settled a bit, a rousing ecumenical group invited me to travel the State, talking in churches and synagogues on the "religious" issues of the presidential campaign of 1984.

So, we formed a Political Action Committee called "Religious Issues '84" and I stumped the State for the next five months, insisting that the real religious issues of the campaign were not prayer in the schools and abortion and homosexuals—as Reagan and the Catholic bishops would have had it—but rather, nuclear arms control, intervention in Central America, and budget priorities as they affect the poor and the powerless in this society.

I drafted a statement called "The Real Agenda," which was signed by 42 Jewish and Christian leaders and got very wide circulation in the State. Some pastors and rabbis said my message was too politically divisive for their pulpit, but in other places we developed ongoing committees that we could keep in touch with. The whole venture was for me an exciting and exhausting plunge into electoral politics, and despite what was a dreary outcome on election day, we raised issues that still continue to be with us.

The Sanctuary Movement

In early 1985, I heard about a growing stream of refugees coming over the border from El Salvador and Guatemala, and I got an invitation to come to Tucson for a very exciting meeting of church people involved with them. The government had just indicted sixteen church workers for illegally transporting and harboring Salvadoran and Guatemalan refugees who had fled for their lives across our border.

I had only intended to meet old friends in Tucson and see what was happening. But they knew of my Central American commitments, and in their clamorous meeting they invited me to start the National Sanctuary Defense Fund. Still nursing my wounds from the Commission debacle, it seemed a splendid new beginning for me, and I agreed with enthusiasm.

We needed, of course, to defend the sixteen church people who had been indicted. That seemed obviously the first call. But to declare the exact legal cause of their indictment took some clarification. Why were these church workers criminally liable "for illegally transporting and harboring Salvadorans and Guatemalans who had fled for their lives across our border?"

Because of U.S. support for the Salvadoran and Guatemalan regimes, refugees who fled those countries were not considered by the U.S. to be refugees worthy of shelter. They should rather be forcefully deported as illegal aliens. Consequently, it was a criminal offense to transport, harbor or protect them.

Emotions were running very high around the country, and we thought that there would be a very long trial, almost certain appeals, and a high probability of further indictments by the government. The legal defense costs, even with half of the top-flight attorneys contributing their services, would surely be more than projected, and then we also needed to protect other incoming refugees from being deported, and help transport them to Sanctuary churches and synagogues around the country.

Sanctuary was not a civil disobedience movement; we were not breaking the law. Rather it was the Justice Department and the Immigration Service who were refusing to allow our Central American refugees the rights which they clearly had under the U.S. Refugee Act of 1980, and that was what we were trying to get before a jury in Federal Court in Tucson. We had a bursting roster to keep us in touch with a national interfaith circuit, helping them to shelter refugees and their families as they came across the border and were sent along the Underground Railroad by the church folks in Tucson.

Just then, out of the blue, I got a phone call from a man named Bernie Mazel. Bernie was a rather elderly seasoned radical, and he was very successful in direct-mail fund-raising, but he was always proud to insist that it was only for progressive causes. He called me saying he had heard about the Sanctuary Movement and thought it was perfect for direct-mail fundraising.

In an offer I couldn't refuse, Bernie said he would write the fundraising letter, print it and mail it to 400,000 people around the country without charge, predicting we would make at least $100,000. We did considerably better than that. Between Bernie's direct mail and foundations, the Sanctuary Defense Fund raised nearly $1.9 million in about nine months, and that went a very long way.

I spent a good part of that first year deeply involved with the trial of the sixteen Sanctuary workers. I was back and forth several times to their courtroom in Tucson, and I tried to interpret what was happening there to the media and to our support network around the country. I opened a simple office at 1610 Bush Street, six blocks from home in San Francisco, hired two wonderful community organizers named Penny Deleray and Eileen Purcell, and we went back and forth to El Salvador for two years. It was a deeply rewarding experience to work with so many remarkable people nationally and internationally.

The Sanctuary movement involved about 250 Protestant, Catholic, Quaker and Jewish congregations around the country, all of whom had declared that they would protect Salvadoran and Guatemalan refugees from being deported by our government. A number of cities also declared themselves Cities of Refuge, and that was exciting to watch.

It was a very vital movement which moved rapidly beyond the trial of the sixteen Sanctuary workers in Tucson in 1984. It fleshed out, for several years thereafter, into a clearinghouse for the national faith-based community around all kinds of immigrant and refugee issues, and I can still feel its excitement. Unprecedented numbers of Americans became involved through their churches and synagogues which proclaimed themselves "sanctuaries."

We had wonderful art shows sponsored by churches, and overflowing fundraiser concerts with Joan Baez, Jackson Browne and Bonnie Raitt. Two of the earliest Tucson organizers of local sanctuaries, Quaker Jim Corbett and John Fife, the pastor of Southside Presbyterian Church in Tucson, were among the fourteen indicted, and they became household names in the movement. And I am delighted today, even honored, to share memories of those days with a new Pilgrim Place resident, Darlene Nicgorski, who was also one of those convicted of feloniously harboring those refugees. I am thrilled to have helped provide funds for her legal defense. And I am still deeply moved to have had a part in such a totally marvelous adventure.

Jumping ahead a bit, I went down to El Salvador twice in 1986, for a week in March to lead a delegation of religious leaders to the refugee camps, and then again in November for a peace conference called by a coalition of trade unionists, teachers and peasants. The tragedy of an earthquake in San Salvador, on top of so much other suffering, was almost beyond description.

I talked to many refugees before they actually got on the trail to come to the United States. I remember one very old and bearded refugee man in tears telling me, "I remember the sufferings of Jesus on his way to the cross and I am part of those sufferings, and that's the only thing that really keeps me going in this camp." To accompany such terrible pain became even more urgent for me. But I haven't been back to El Salvador since 1990.

To China

In September of 1985, our friend Bernie Mazel invited Donna and me to go on an eighteen-day trip to China with a group of ten "Peacemakers." That was a wonderful change of pace, and we had long wanted to go to China. We were official guests of the Chinese government, of all things, and the group included Cora and Peter Weiss as well as Bill and Randy Coffin. We met with all sorts of government officials, and we talked to many local groups wanting to meet with Americans. Bill Coffin always found his way to a piano to tinkle the keys and delight our audiences, particularly the children, wherever he could.

My overwhelming challenge was trying to realize what a population of one billion Chinese means. How do you create a social and political system for almost one quarter of the human race? The new opening to the West and to private economic initiative in China had generated enormous enthusiasm, and that was a fascinating experiment to watch developing.

Donna and I had a wonderful stroll along the Great Wall, which was a very steep climb and a good workout for us. And I can still remember standing under the famous picture of Mao at Tiananmen Square in the center of Beijing, with throngs of people, old and young, gracefully doing their Tai Chi among the fluttering pigeons all around us.

We found the Chinese on hordes of bicycles everywhere we went. The bicycles at 7:30 AM were not to be believed. They were so civil. No hurry, no arguments, no accidents, all bikes going at the same smooth speed, almost meditatively. But it was still an exciting challenge to weave between the silent throngs of bicycles to get across the street. These bicycles were, of course, sadly modernized into hordes of traffic-clogging cars and trucks by the time we visited China again some years later.

Bernie Mazel was a very generous host, and he gave us a wonderful introduction to the country. We met some very fascinating people as official guests of the Chinese government, and the Coffins and Cora and Peter Weiss were delightful companions, always with provocative insights. That splendid introduction stood us in good stead when we returned to China in 2001.

Wanting to get off the activist circuit for a while, I began to do some quiet writing about the challenge of liberation that I had experienced in Central America. Just then, someone directed me to Harper's in San Francisco, and we talked about a book on my work in liberation theology that I would start to write. I was emotionally exhausted from the sagas I had been through, and that book still remains to be written, although these memoirs might just be a challenge to again look into it.

Stanford Dean of the Chapel

In the fall of 1986, by a wonderful return of the karmic cycle, I was appointed by Stanford University President Donald Kennedy to be Interim Dean of the Chapel at Stanford. I was pastor of the University Church and Dean of Religious Affairs for the whole university, and I was proud to stand in a long line of Deans which included such distinguished dear friends and colleagues as Davie Napier and Robert McAfee Brown. Davie had a great reputation as an outstanding Dean during the turbulent '60s, and it was often awesome to hear of his majestic achievements in my office in the Round Room.

It was also a special blessing of all this time to get to know better and love Bob Brown and his wife, Sydney Thomson Brown. After a great career at Union Theological Seminary in New York, Bob had been a very popular Dean of the Chapel and a dynamic teacher and activist as a Professor of Religion some years earlier.

We had many common interests, especially in ecumenism, which was still new in those years, and in Central America and Liberation Theology. Bob was a great hero to many Stanford students, and it was a joy for me to follow him around the student body. Sydney was committed to many more social justice issues than I could ever keep my eye on, as I believe she still is to this day.

Bob Brown died in 2001, but he remains a moving spirit in my life. William Sloane Coffin was a close friend of Bob and wrote the introduction to his Memoirs, *Reflections Over the Long Haul* (Westminster Press, 2005). In it Coffin said of Bob Brown, "In his company we tended to be our better selves." Bob drew out all the best in those around him, and I have always wished that such a wonderful tribute might someday stand on my own tombstone.

From my notes in our job interview in the President's

office, I remember Donald Kennedy saying to me, "Besides relating Memorial Church to all the departments of the University, I want someone to be Dean of the Chapel who will encourage students to have a sense of public service and get to work outside their own backyard. From your record, I think you could do that all across the university." I thrived on roaming through the university with that mandate, bridging the Chapel with many academic disciplines as well as with all kinds of justice and political issues in the wider community. In fact, I often recall Kennedy's call to "get to work outside your own back yard" when I talk with students today.

Donna and I rented out our place in San Francisco and took a small apartment on campus for a year. Although I had never regularly preached before, I was especially glad to preach every Sunday in Memorial Church on the stately Quadrangle. By the terms of their will, Leland Stanford, Jr., and his wife, Jane, had originally insisted that Memorial Church be a non-denominational Christian church, and I was conscious of that every time I led worship and mounted the great pulpit.

But I suspect that my vision of what radical religious values could mean in the life of a great university was just more of a challenge than Stanford wanted to take on, and it made some people uneasy. I wasn't easily definable as a priestly person, rather than an ecclesiastical parson; and after a year it was not surprising that a more conventional permanent Dean was appointed.

Still, I had a chance to say some valuable things from that Stanford platform, and to do some good work. It brought together much of my teaching and priestly ministry of the previous fifteen years, and put it in a centered focus in a great university. It all felt just fine, a wonderful gift and an adventure in ministry that I would not have missed for anything.

Then, on the invitation of some dear English friends, Martin and Ruth Conway, Donna and I took some time off and spent six quiet weeks in their home in Oxford. Donna audited a course at the University on the British health system and I just hung out. Besides hiking in the Cotswolds and roaming the gorgeous countryside around Oxford, we had a welcome time of rest and reading. We walked the winding quiet streets amid bustling students in their caps and gowns, and went into London for some music and theater.

On a beautiful afternoon, we even went punting on the Thames, which was a real kick. In August, we drove up to Scotland for a marvelous week on the Isle of Iona, a weekend with old Grail friend Anne Mathews in Edinburgh just at Festival time, and a glorious family celebration of the 70th birthday of our dear friend, Rita Lockhart, in Ayr. It was all a fine transition to the new horizons which were awaiting me.

Food First

In September of 1987 we landed back in San Francisco, and I was appointed the Executive Director of the Institute for Food and Development Policy, an international research and education center better known

as Food First. Founded by Joseph Collins and Frances
Moore Lappé in 1975, after she had published *Diet for a
Small Planet*, (which later sold three million copies), the
Institute went to work on all the root causes of why there
are so many hungry people in a world of such plenty.
It was good work, but the organization was in terrible
disarray.

Frankie Lappé had run Food First as a commune for
more than ten years. Everyone sat in a circle and made
decisions together. That was very fashionable then, and
they went broke about four times. After much discussion,
and with great fanfare, I was now to be their first Executive Director.

I was honored, but a little shaky about what I was
getting into, so I insisted that I would come only if these
two founding stars would become staff members respon-
sible to me just like all the other staff members under my
leadership. They agreed and it became a very exciting
three years.

It was a perfect fit for me: broad international issues,
a staff of eighteen wonderful people with a very progressive analysis, some eighty titles on our publications list, a
budget of $1.2 million to administer, and a platform from
which I could speak out on most of the justice and political issues I really care about. We had 20,000 members
from around the world who provided 70% of our budget,
and the rest had to be raised from grant proposals which I
was expected to write.

The issue of food is obviously a central one, and I
found it terribly complex. Frances Moore Lappé used to

say, as she still says today, that there already is enough food in the world to feed every human being a diet of 3,000 calories a day. The problem is distribution and the turning of food into a market commodity in the capitalist system. It was for me an even deeper immersion into the ravages of Empire.

I found that food and hunger offered great possibilities for broad community organizing. I had a dynamic staff, including a warm good friend, Walden Bello, a Filipino international activist of some renown. Naomi Klein had once called Walden Bello "the world's leading no-nonsense revolutionary," and he later became a member of the Philippine House of Representatives.

With Walden's help, Donna and I went to the Philippines in 1988 and 1989. Sponsored by PATH, (Philippine Assistance for Technology and Health), good meetings were arranged for us with leaders and ordinary folks from every sector and political persuasion in the post-Marcos Philippines society. We met with women who had been imprisoned and tortured under the Marcos regime, and we spent some time visiting the grinding poverty and gruesome stench of Smokey Mountain in the center of Manila.

I kept remarking on parallels I was seeing between the Philippines and what I had seen in El Salvador. Cory Aquino was a woman of great integrity, but she was almost totally controlled by the military and by the landowners and business elites—a new set of "cronies," but not much different from the bad old Marcos days.

Government-sanctioned Vigilantes—what Salvadorans

called "death squads" roamed the streets in the name of rabid anti-Communism. Peasants were being bombed out of their villages, and no real land reform was in sight. And the support of the United States for all this, in its huge military bases and its economic and political and social presence everywhere, seemed to me more direct and immediate than in any other country in the world.

On each of our trips, Walden sent us to visit with the sugar cane workers on the island of Negros. All bloody from slashing the cane, the workers were organizing against their bosses who were taking payments out of their pay for health insurance without ever turning that money in for the workers to receive their health care. It was a dismal and brutal scene. Our visits to Negros moved me deeply, but I saw little chance of any justice ever coming to those cane workers.

On Negros, we met with a wonderful Irish missionary, Niall O'Brien, author of the remarkable book, *Revolution From The Heart* (Oxford, 1987). For more than thirty years, Niall O'Brien fought valiantly for social justice among the Filipino peasants, and it was exciting to hear of his work. He died in 2004 at age 64, and his name is honored today among the heroes in the Philippines. I later became involved in Philippines support work back home, giving talks and hosting Filipino visitors, and I still try to keep in contact with that very beautiful land.

Not long after our time in the Philippines, I went to Honduras and Nicaragua for two weeks, leading young people on what Food First called a "Reality Tour." We had set up Reality Tours to focus on the low-to-the-ground connection between action and reflection, probing ever more sharply into the radical social analysis of Paulo Freire.

I was more convinced than ever that Ronald Reagan's support for the Contras in Nicaragua was just a disgrace, with no relation whatever to "freedom fighters" or the great traditions of our country. At the time, there was enormous energy running in Central America for the celebrated Peace Plan of Mortimer Arias, the radical Methodist Bishop in Bolivia, and I found Washington to be the major obstacle to the whole peace process.

In October of 1989, Donna and I had a remarkable three-week Asian journey. After travelling briefly to Japan, including a wonderful few days in Kyoto, I represented Food First and was invited to speak on poverty and hunger at a World Congress of the International Physicians for the Prevention of Nuclear War, which was held in the Peace Park in Hiroshima.

It was a first-class event, bringing together physicians from all over the world, and we were right at the dramatic site of the nuclear blast memorial, with a powerful museum and some stark ruins surrounding us. I remember that Los Angeles Rabbi Leonard Beerman was there, and that he led an observance of Yom Kippur, with a focus on repentance for the 1945 bombing of Hiroshima.

Besides sharing that profound experience of 3,000 doctors from 72 countries convening in such a dramatic place to call for an end to nuclear war, Donna and I were delighted to spend that week in Hiroshima living in the home of a Japanese doctor, his wife and their two young children.

The doctor was the only one who spoke English, and we appreciated the warm hospitality of his lovely and laughing family. They were fantastic hosts, and the night before we left, the children gave us stick drawings they had made of us—very tall people in their eyes! And then they all went joyfully with us to the train station, as we went on to Tokyo.

From Japan, we went back to the Philippines, again for a week with friends working with the sugar workers and internal refugees on Negros. We were disturbed even more than we had been a year earlier by the poverty and injustice that was everywhere the lot of the Filipino peasant, even under the U.S-supported regime of Cory Aquino.

After hunkering down in our hotel room for 36 very long hours in a raging typhoon in Manila, we then went on to Taiwan, where I had been invited to give a major address in Taipei on "Environment, Development and Values." Donna ended up also giving an unplanned address at the same event on "Issues of Aging," sparking a fascinating discussion with physicians on East-West approaches to the reality of aging and the care of elders in our societies.

We stayed in the Taiwan YWCA, and I shall never forget sitting in our room watching the first graphic pictures of the big Loma Prieta earthquake which had just struck the Bay Area on October 19. That 1989 quake was also known as the "World Series Earthquake," marking the exact time on which it hit and froze the San Francisco ball park during the World Series game.

We watched lots of it on TV, nervously looking for our own roof in San Francisco. We felt very far from home, but when we got home a few days later, we were anxious but then relieved to find that only a few pictures had fallen off the wall and all was well with our friends.

That trip was really my swan song at Food First. I resigned my position in December, 1989, when the founders of that organization, particularly Frances Moore Lappé, changed its whole direction, and I could no longer do what I had been hired to do and was doing with such enthusiasm for almost three years.

I have always been deeply grateful to have been part of that exciting Food First venture. Once when I was flying on a plane, a very portly man sitting next to me asked me what I did. I replied that I was the Director of Food First. He put down his martini and said, "Oh, I know that lefty crowd. They're the ones who say that we have a right to eat. These lefties are creating rights all over the place, and now we have a right to eat!" Food First was a very challenging and satisfying time, and I always felt it was really good work.

El Salvador

One of my great delights in 1990 was to chair the Board of the New El Salvador Today Foundation (NEST), and in that capacity I led a small delegation of leading church members to El Salvador for a week in

February, which turned out to be a very turbulent time there. Our purpose was originally to look at some grassroots medical clinics and neighborhood development projects which NEST was supporting in El Salvador, to see what help we might be.

But we stayed in the same hotel in San Salvador with a Congressional delegation, the Moakley Committee, and their concerns completely changed our mission. They were investigating the recent deaths of six Jesuits, their housekeeper and her daughter, who had been viciously murdered some months earlier outside the Jesuit University of the Central Americas, the UCA.

It was very valuable to talk with the Congress members as they went on their rounds from President Alfredo Cristiani to the military High Command to the UCA and to the American Embassy. Our delegation followed the same route right after them, and we got deeply into the investigation of the murders.

I was profoundly moved by our visit to the UCA, and to the simple community house that had housed my six Jesuit brothers, including a good friend of mine, Ignacio Ellacuria, who was the country's leading intellectual and Rector of the UCA. They had been slaughtered by the U.S. trained death squad named the Atlacatl Counterinsurgency Battalion, using U.S. bullets and wearing full military uniforms bought with the money of U.S. taxpayers.

Somehow it just outraged me that the death squad had dragged the priests and the two women from their beds out into the courtyard, with the indignity of still being in their nightshirts and bare feet. And before shooting them, they had gouged their eyes out, which they said was to teach them a lesson about seeing too much.

Just before we arrived in 1990, Salvadoran President Alfredo Cristiani had famously come to Harvard to watch his son play squash against Princeton, and he was met by demonstrators who shouted "death squad president" outside the gym. Later, in January of 1992, Cristiani and ten leftist guerrilla generals signed a treaty ending the bloody twelve-year conflict.

In 1993, a UN report blamed the civil war crimes in El Salvador on the state security forces, but Cristiani criticized the report and rejected it, saying it would not contribute to healing his country's wounds. In that same year, his own right wing Party, Arena, pushed through a blanket amnesty of all Salvadorans who had committed political murder and other crimes during the twelve years of civil war, and Cristiani was exonerated. Case closed.

Somehow, the violent wretchedness of it all simply infuriated me as I heard other Jesuits tell of the murders, and I still recall it vividly. I had studied for four years in Innsbruck with Ignacio Ellacuria, the Rector of the UCA, and I remember being ordained lying right by his side in the University Church in Innsbruck in 1960. He had been a man of great style. I also knew and had corresponded with Segundo Montes, a remarkable priest and sociologist who was also murdered. It moved me to tears to touch their blood still spattered on the walls of their simple rooms. And I still carry their pictures over my desk here as I write.

The Quakers

In 1991 and 1992, the AFSC asked me to work on organizational issues and program development for the their offices in San Francisco and Atlanta. I had long valued the many peace projects of the Quakers and also the whole ethos of the Quaker community. To reverence "That of God" in all persons and in all things is the Quaker vision, and that resonates exceedingly well with my incarnational theology.

The San Francisco office was a particular challenge. The prior executive, whom I knew, had resigned abruptly under the strain of some serious financial and personnel problems. I had a staff of thirty, a budget of $3 million, and marvelous social justice programs throughout Northern California.

Along with leading a national search for a new Director, I had to manage a process for budget cuts of $120,000, which meant "laying down" three programs and three staff. Quakers don't "cut" programs and staff. They "lay them down." That somehow seems non-violent and more humane, implying that all might be raised up again if the money ever returns.

I visited Quaker meetings regularly in California and later in Georgia, and began to appreciate the Spirit-filled and non-directive decision-making process of the Quakers. As a liberation theologian, I was intrigued to see that Quaker process has a vital and very effective "liberation" commitment, with no explicit "theology" needed. I saw it as a kind of "low church" liberation theology, and it somehow took me full circle theologically. Quaker process was, and still remains for me, a remarkable stretch in my own faith journey.

A great example was at my first national board meeting in Philadelphia, the first of five such meetings I attended there. In the colonial motherhouse of all Quaker meetings on red-brick Cherry Street, the seventy members from Friends Meetings all over the country and numerous lawyers from the international Friends Service Committee had an urgent agenda item. We needed to discuss what the penalties would be if the AFSC did not obey the recent Justice Department requirement that the Service Committee demand I-9 Employment Registration Forms from every staff member whom we hired.

I was fascinated by my first up-close view of Quaker process. Not a lot of doctrinal discussion, but lots of prayerful silence before serious decisions are taken. People would stand and speak briefly on this very serious issue of demanding I-9 Forms that could possibly mean the end of the AFSC. And then they would simply sit down, rather than elaborate their ideas or comment on the ideas of others.

At one point, after a moment of silence, the Clerk simply declared that it seemed clear to her that there was consensus in the meeting, and that the Service Committee would continue to be in non-compliance with the law on I-9 Forms, insisting that Quakers were on the side of workers, and particularly on the side of immigrant workers, and they were not going to do the government's work for them.

This was a question of the very survival of the AFSC
and its world-wide work, but the mind of the assembly
seemed obvious to everyone, so no further discussion or
formal vote was needed. As a Liberation Theologian, I
remain a great admirer of the Quaker spirit of peace and
spiritual power in their very serious justice commitments.

I was somewhat out of breath from the pace, but
together with lots of wonderful Quakers around me, my
time in the San Francisco Regional Office seemed to
come off pretty well; and, after a two-year search, we finally called a courageous and charismatic leader named
Wilson Riles, Jr. to take over, which he did with great
acclaim.

Not long after I finished in San Francisco, the Service Committee asked me to go to Atlanta, where there
were also difficulties in their staff and the Regional
Director had quit. I would bring some order in the staff
and programs, and again run a national search for a new
director.

I agreed to go, but, stretched thin as Donna and I
both were, only if I could fly back to San Francisco or
Donna could fly to Atlanta for some quiet time every
other weekend. They agreed and I was there for eight or
nine months, enjoying the generous hospitality of Emory
professor and old Jesuit compañero Cene Bianchi, and
his future wife, Peggy Hermann, and exploring the whole
new world of Georgia politics and political concerns.

For several years during all this time, Donna and I
were fed and supported by a Base Christian Community of about twelve people that met monthly in our San

Francisco living room for a meal and some prayer and quiet reflection on our common concerns and commitments. Among others, the group included Bob and Sydney Brown, several Quakers and Methodists, a Catholic priest and a former nun. We called ourselves the "Compas," the Compañeros/as, and that rich experience was the closest thing we had ever had to real church, and we were very grateful for our time together. That community filled a critical need in our lives, and we continued to meet with them for many years thereafter, until we moved to Claremont.

And we were also nourished by regular visits to the Benedictine Abbey at Whitethorn, about three hundred miles up in the gorgeous redwood forests along the California coast. We would just retreat there for some wonderful silence with the cloistered sisters from time to time, and for many years we celebrated Holy Week and Easter with them in a very creative liturgy looking out onto the redwood giants all around us. Several of those remarkable women became our dear friends, and we're still in touch with them.

South Africa

In 1989, just before Nelson Mandela was freed from prison on Robben Island, we had a treasured visit from a dear South African friend, Anne Hope, who was about to return to South Africa after 17 years in exile. Anne said she would be living in Cape Town, and she convinced us with great enthusiasm that we should come there, since

South Africa was then the most exciting country in all the world. And she said that we should come for at least two years, if we came at all.

But before we decided to take on South Africa for two years, we thought we should come first to look around, so in the winter of 1992, we spent an exploratory three weeks in Cape Town, Johannesburg and Durban. Anne Hope graciously showed us about, and we visited widely, especially in the gorgeous Cape Province.

We also spent two days in Soweto, an enormous township of three million (!) squatters, of varied income levels, even seeing Nelson Mandela's simple little house among the hovels. There were no street names or house numbers, and we visited the huge general hospital for the whole township, called Baragwanath. Donna got to meet some of the women of Black Sash, and the leaders of the National Legal Resources Centre, and that served as her opening for some good work when we returned to Cape Town the following year.

We finally decided to spend all of 1993 and 1994 in South Africa, sixteen months before the election of Nelson Mandela as President and eight months after, and it was the most profound intercultural experience of our lives.

Before we could start out, however, we first had to find a way to support our pilgrim selves for two years, and that turned into an adventure all its own. We didn't want to take jobs away from South Africans, and the church and civic groups that Anne had connected us with in Cape Town couldn't afford to pay us, since most of their money came from overseas and those funds were dwindling in the post-apartheid era.

I was planning to do some research in the Religious Studies Department at the University of Cape Town, and there didn't seem to be any funding for that. So we sent grant proposals to six major foundations. These were not successful, but Donna submitted a Fulbright Grant application, and that happily came through with funding for our second year. That was a great start.

Then the Tides Foundation in San Francisco (which couldn't give us any direct funding) set us up as a quasi-501c3 project of our own, to which we gave the catchy name of VISA, Volunteers in South Africa. Donna wrote a very persuasive letter to our 900 closest friends and relatives, asking for some financial help with our volunteer work, in return for which they would get regular reports from us on our work in South Africa.

We said that we were not going to South Africa to "help," but rather that South Africa had far more to teach us than we could ever bring there. We really took that seriously, and we got 360 responses from our wonderful VISA network, bringing us $35,000 in contributions. That would cover most of our travel and expenses for our first year, so with the Fulbright grant to cover our second year, we were on our way.

To each of those who had responded to our VISA call we sent a quarterly newsletter from Cape Town for the next two years, creating a unique network of information, energy and commitments. We mailed these letters off to Pasadena, where they were graciously sent out by Claire

Gorfinkel. Claire is a dear friend, and, more recently, the publisher of these Memoirs.

We rented a beautiful, somewhat funky, Cape Victorian house, owned by the foremost Quaker in South Africa, Hendrik van der Merwe, simply known as "HV," or "Hah Ver" in Afrikaans. His deceased wife, Marietje, had been a potter of some renown, and the house was full of lots of her beautiful African art.

HV had just retired as the founding director of the Centre for Intergroup Studies in Cape Town, renowned for its work on mediation in interracial struggles; and he was about to go off to Washington for a year as a Fellow at the newly-founded U.S. Institute of Peace, to work on the tortured question of restitution for victims of apartheid in South Africa.

With community development workers in Soweto, South Africa, 1992

The house was in a leafy corner of Cape Town known as Observatory. From our window, we had a beautiful view of the 3,000-ft. Devil's Peak out over the Bay, and I became a Senior Research Fellow in Religious Studies at the University of Cape Town. We loved the quiet beauty of the place, and set about exploring this exciting new city.

Cape Town is about 900 miles southwest of Johannesburg. Right after arriving, we hiked for several hours down the edge of the Cape Coast to the magnificent Cape Point. We were standing right at the southern tip of the whole continent of Africa, and I remember being thrilled to look out at the mysterious, roiling confluence of the Indian Ocean and the Atlantic Ocean.

An arrow on a little wooden post told us that we were exactly 10,341 miles due East of San Francisco, and when we learned that airmail letters would take two weeks to get there (so it was in those days!), we knew that we were very far away from home and on an awesome new adventure.

Anne Hope and her partner, Sally Timmel, opened many doors for us when we arrived. They had published their "Training for Transformation," a very successful three-volume manual for community organizers, and they were out on the road all over Southern Africa with that.

We were delighted to learn that Anne and Sally were recently married in Cape Town, and that they will hopefully soon become residents with us here at Pilgrim Place. They will make a great addition to our community, and we look forward to returning their gracious welcome to us when we needed it so badly.

The Legal Resources Centre was a non-profit national public interest law program modeled after the NAACP Legal Defense Fund in the United States, and it primarily assisted black and mixed race South Africans.

The LRC had offices in the six major South African cities, and its focus was to pursue justice and human rights, particularly for blacks. It had been founded by Arthur Chaskalson, who was a member of the legal defense team for Nelson Mandela in the famous Rivonia Trial of 1963.

Arthur Chaskalson later became the celebrated first Chief Justice of the post-apartheid Constitutional Court. He had been introduced to us by our long-time friend, Clinton Bamberger, a renowned human rights attorney in Baltimore, and he died in 2012. We are very proud to have known him.

The LRC did critically important work, and Donna was excited to be with them. She also had an opportunity to work with Black Sash, the courageous national organization of white women who had for decades fought apartheid and risked detention or banning for their activities. Their name comes from their custom of wearing a black sash as a sign of mourning for the death of the South African Constitution as they stood in silence at demonstrations.

Black Sash was a great place for Donna to carry out her Fulbright Grant for the second year, to research income sources for elderly people of color in South Africa, and I also did a little work with them on interracial issues, proud to be with a such dynamic group of progressive women.

We certainly felt continuing violence all around us. For example, there was a terrorist massacre during a service in a church nearby, and another massacre in a pub just around our corner. But our experience from the beginning in Cape Town was that there was almost no interracial stress on the streets themselves. There was a mysterious calm as we walked about, and I remember being deeply moved by that.

I remember so well that, unlike my experience in this country, I easily made eye contact with people of color on the streets of Cape Town, and smiles came from them easily. Blacks were clearly the overwhelming majority, and therefore they enjoyed a certain self-confidence in knowing that they were at home in their own country, but, still, I knew that something very special was going on here as we passed one another.

Warmed by all this, one of my central projects, in fact my obsession during my whole time there, was to under-stand what South Africans mean by their goal of a "non-racial South Africa." Since the birth of the post-apartheid era, South Africans have asserted that "race will not be a determinant factor" in public policy and social life in South Africa.

For anyone sensitive to the history of the civil rights struggle in the United States, the ideology of "non-racial-ism" is bound to be somewhat startling. At least it was for me. Not multi-racial or inter-racial or multi-cultural equality, but the vision is of a society which, in all its political and economic and social institutions, is simply non-racial, full-stop. Is this really for real, I wondered, or is it only verbal gymnastics?

In 1955, an historic Congress of the People—Black Africans, Indians, Coloreds (or mixed race), and Whites—had drafted the Freedom Charter, projecting a magnificent vision of a future South Africa after the defeat of apartheid.

Its opening affirmation enshrined the enduring vision of a non-racial democratic state: "South Africa belongs to all who live in it, black and white." Nelson Mandela often repeated this mantra after his election, assuring nervous whites that they need not flee the country, as many did following other black liberation movements across Africa.

The months leading up to the election of Nelson Mandela on April 27, 1994 were a time of enormous tension, boundless hopes, racial violence and huge manic-depressive swings of public mood. As a prelude to leaving the country, many liberal whites were saying that the wounds of apartheid injustice were simply so deep and so festering that no new democratically elected regime, even the African National Congress, with an overwhelming mandate on election day, could bring sufficient healing fast enough to stay in power for long.

We saw a lot of troubling truth to that. In our time, South Africa's five million whites were about fifteen percent of the country's forty million people. They owned eighty-five percent of the land and controlled ninety-eight percent of the wealth of the country.

More than eighty-five percent of all South Africans were black, or simply "African," as they were called. Starting in 1948, the deliberate apartheid denial of basic social services to this overwhelming majority of about thirty-four million black people was accompanied by the creation of a world of very sophisticated services, virtually a welfare state, for the white minority.

In our years, only one in four black families in greater Cape Town lived in formal housing, seventy-five percent of them squatters. I can remember wandering endlessly one day while searching for people in nearby Khayelitsha, a vast township of 400,000 blacks, mostly recent immigrants from the Transkei. That was an enormous community of homeless peasants strewn out on the sandy flats outside Cape Town.

They were living in tin or tarpaper shacks randomly strewn about on dirt tracks, with no postal delivery system and almost no local health care services. I can only presume that the living conditions in Khayelitsha today are even more crowded and impoverished. The New South Africa since Nelson Mandela may have changed at least a bit of that, but, given the horrendous destitution we saw, it still must be much the same.

Nationally, ninety percent of all African families were without any electricity, and seven million lacked easy access to potable water. Seventeen million Africans, or fifty percent of all blacks, lived below the poverty line. As an outsider and white, it was really impossible for me to appreciate the pain and injustice which those terrible figures described.

As the country approached its first election, two major incidents threatened to shatter the shining dream of a non-racial democracy. The first was the assassination of Chris Hani by a white terrorist. He was the second most beloved black leader after Nelson Mandela, and he was a hero to many. And the second was the violent murder of a young white woman named Amy Biehl by blacks in Guguletu, a township just down the road from us.

Both of these tragedies were of enormous importance in the crisis of rebirth of the nation, and each was one of those events where people will always remember where they were when they first heard the news.

Chris Hani was assassinated in front of his home between Good Friday and Easter Sunday in 1993, in the dark between crucifixion and resurrection. I remember that Cape Town was very still that evening as we drove down to the Midnight Easter Vigil in St. George's Cathedral.

After the new fire was struck in the dark of the crowded cathedral, it was just soul-shattering to hear the strong voice of Archbishop Desmond Tutu ring out of the motionless silence: "I loved Chris Hani." I can still see him and hear him to this day.

Tutu's somber and grieving homily touched us deeply, in that church that had been such a center of the liberation struggle for the blacks of South Africa. Four black infants were brought to baptism in the middle of the liturgy, and it was only in holding and hugging them as he sprinkled them that the famous Desmond Tutu smile began to come alive again. It was a very moving celebration of the Easter mystery.

"Comrade" Chris Hani was an extraordinary black leader and a charismatic figure of very special quality. At his death he was General Secretary of the South African Communist Party, and he had been a celebrated chief-of-staff of umKonto we Sizwe, or MK, the military arm of the ANC.

One of Chris Hani's funeral orators hailed him as a "subtle and scholarly soldier and a compassionate and committed Communist." He had a special, compelling appeal to the "young lions," the lost generation of militant youth who lived by rage and violence in the wastelands that were the black townships. And he nurtured as best he could the MK's deep commitment to non-violence, but that fact was rarely mentioned or ever really understood.

In a certain sense, the blacks of South Africa became visible for the first time during Chris Hani's funeral. They passed from shadow to sharp focus in the eyes of many whites. The live radio broadcast of those deeply moving events, which we heard, forced many white South Africans to face the reality of a radical passage of power in the country, and the political landscape shifted with a tangible jolt.

Apartheid was built on what white Afrikaners considered a divinely mandated network of institutions whose goal was the isolation and alienation of one race from another—geographically, economically and spiritually. The black township was always out on the edge of town, tucked away just over the hill.

We had often remarked that, outside of the major urban centers in South Africa, one could drive for miles through towns and villages and hardly realize that blacks lived there at all. It was always easy to shut one's eyes to what went on in the townships—the squalor, the indignity, the hopelessness, the angry violence that became a way of life.

But the visibility of the black masses at Chris Hani's funeral made it clear to all South Africans that they could no longer separate themselves from this wretched aftermath of apartheid, and the national goal of building a non-racial democracy took on an immense new clarity and vigor.

The other great setback for the dream of non-racialism was the murder in August of a young American woman, Amy Biehl, in Guguletu, the black township about ten minutes from our house.

Amy Biehl had been a recent graduate of Stanford University, where she had written the words "Free Mandela" on her graduation mortarboard. An anti-apartheid activist, she was about to return home after a Fulbright grant at the University of the Western Cape. A very attractive blonde, bright, committed and street-smart, she was an altogether remarkable person.

Her commitment was to empower black youth in the challenged and vulnerable black townships within the Western Cape. For us and for many South Africans, black and white, the most disturbing thing about her death was the overt racist motivation in it, particularly

121

when Amy herself had found such a non-racial way of living.

Amy was driving three black friends home to Guguletu. She was stoned and dragged out of her car and beaten by a black mob because she was white—because she was a "settler," they said. Even her black friends whom she was driving home that evening couldn't reason with the roaring mob by the side of the dusty road.

The whole thing was deeply sad and tragic—not just for Amy Biehl and those who loved her, but for the great shining vision of a non-racial democratic society which had driven the South African liberation struggle for decades.

Amy Biehl was of a wealthy Newport Beach family and her staunch Republican parents, Linda and Peter, came to Cape Town and Guguletu soon after her murder, to say, in very moving ceremonies, that they forgave those who had killed their daughter.

The Biehls established a foundation in their daughter's name, to support the education and development of black South Africans, especially in Guguletu. The four black youth who were sentenced for Amy's murder later got amnesty from the Truth and Reconciliation Commission in 1998, and the Amy Biehl Foundation is still a vital service program for youth in Guguletu and the surrounding townships.

The Biehls have also built the Amy Biehl High School in Albuquerque, which is very imaginative and thriving today, carrying out Amy's commitments to empower black youth. CBS News did Amy's story on 60

Minutes in January of 1994, not long after her murder. The Amy Biehl Foundation website is well worth a visit. It is both informative and inspirational in describing Amy's great work, which still continues long after her.

While working in the Religious Studies Department at the University of Cape Town, I was often breathless with the number of intriguing projects that kept coming to my attention. The first one I chose engrossed me completely. With focus groups in the townships, I travelled widely on a project called "Theology and Economic Values in the New South Africa," which I had created with the help of several colleagues at the University.

It was fascinating going into the townships; and in informal discussion groups I would ask people why they were doing what they were doing, probing to help them see some theological values in their work.

I remember once asking a man in Khayelitsha why he was bringing food to hungry people. He answered that he thought that was a dumb question. "I do it because they are hungry," he said. And then, in our circle we would try quietly to discern some deeper theological or spiritual values in his hunger work. And so it went with others working on all sorts of burning poverty issues.

I also designed a broader, two-year research project called "Non-Racialism and Multi-Culturalism: South Africa and the United States," to be carried out in the Religious Studies Department. That brought me into rich and close contact with three wonderful colleagues at the University.

Barney Pityana is a renowned human rights lawyer

and theologian who had been an associate with anti-apartheid activist Steve Biko in founding the Black Consciousness Movement in the 1970's, and he had also founded the Programme to Combat Racism at the World Council of Churches. Charles Villa-Vicencio and John de Gruchy are both superb theologians and well-known names in the antiapartheid struggle.

Charles Villa-Vicencio later became Research Director for the Truth and Reconciliation Commission, and he worked very closely with Desmond Tutu in establishing ways to bring together apartheid oppressors and their victims in the painful call to national reconciliation. I only recently discovered that Charles has for some years now been a Fellow at the Woodstock Center and the Berkley Center for Religion, Peace and World Affairs at Georgetown University in Washington. I value very highly the friendship I enjoyed with him and his colleagues, and I hope I might one day be back in touch with him.

Among our many privileges, we were able to share in the frantic anxieties and the wild exhilaration of the election of the country's first democratically elected President, Nelson Mandela, and the birth of a New South Africa in 1994. As some people said, it was "the fairy-tale ending, where the hideous frog of apartheid turns into the handsome prince of non-racial democracy."

Donna and I trained a number of election observers for the election, and it was very moving for us also to be election observers in that historic event, with a line five hours long outside our polling place in a large sports hall. Throngs of excited people came dancing and singing down the line, in the driving rain. It was just a remarkable experience helping these people do what they had been waiting to do all their lives.

In mid-morning, with arms thrown high over his head, Desmond Tutu dashed into the election hall in all his red robes, and simply cried out over the roar of the crowd, "We are the Rainbow People of God. Thanks be to God!" And then he just turned and sped away with a UN observer at his side.

Desmond Tutu really meant that profoundly Christian and Muslim and Jewish affirmation, and most South Africans came to believe him. It somehow took on added meaning as they watched him personally flinching in pain at the stories of torturous inhumanity that later came before the famous Truth and Reconciliation Commission over which he presided.

On our later visit to South Africa in 1999, we attended one of those TRC sessions; and it was an unforgettable experience to watch an elderly Afrikaner come slowly forward to shakily confess that he had tortured and murdered a certain black man, whom he named. Then, in tears, he asked for reconciliation and pleaded for forgiveness from that man's widow, who was sitting crying in the front row. She came up and tearfully gave him a great hug, and the call to reconciliation had worked.

We were deeply privileged to attend the historic opening of South Africa's first democratic Parliament, on May 9, 1994 in Cape Town. When all the newly elected members gathered for the first time in the Great Hall of the Parliament, brand new traditions were spontaneously created, and it was wonderful to watch it all from our balcony seats.

There were unprecedented scenes of African culture, color and warmth, and unrestrained hugging in all directions. The new MPs seemed to go around in search of people to practice national unity on. The difference was not just in the addition of many black members to the Parliament, but in the vast array of women MPs, wearing flamboyant traditional dress. A sense of Africa was in the air, heightened by the entry of the *imbongi,* or praise-singer, in blankets and leopard-skin cap, carrying his traditional weapons and shouting out a torrent of praise for "Madiba," the African clan name of the new President.

We heard thunderous applause and cheers as Nelson Mandela and his two Deputy Presidents, Thabo Mbeki and F.W. de Klerk, came down the aisle shaking hands, American style. Then, four hundred new MPs went up in batches of ten to take their oath of office.

The biggest outburst of applause and *toyi-toyi* dancing through the Great Hall came when the Chief Justice announced Nelson Mandela's unopposed election as President. Women ululated and the Great Hall went jubilant. Five Afrikaner Air Force jets roared overhead, streaming behind them glorious contrails in rainbow colors. And Desmond Tutu cried out once again, "We are the Rainbow People of God!"

An Indian woman was unanimously elected Speaker. Then a prayer was offered in Arabic by a sheikh, and the most amazing parliamentary session in South Africa's history was adjourned. Members of all parties and colors rose, and the hugging began in earnest.

We were thrilled to be a part of that occasion; and, watching it, we felt that it was all going to work. And that magnificent process is still at work today, even though much poverty and interracial tension still remain. The Rainbow Nation of Madiba Mandela was indeed born that day, but the decades of apartheid injustice will still take perhaps many generations to overcome.

One of our most moving encounters in South Africa was a long visit we had with Beyers Naudé, a South African cleric, theologian and leading Afrikaner anti-apartheid activist. He had been defrocked by the Dutch Reformed Church in 1960 when, with a ringing prophetic call from the pulpit, he announced his powerful conviction that apartheid was a sin.

With Beyers Naudé in Johannesburg, South Africa, 1992

Beyers had founded the Christian Institute, which courageously led the anti-apartheid resistance of the churches for more than a decade. He suffered an ugly ostracism from his social and ecclesiastical Afrikaner peers, and he endured long bouts of the strictest kind of banning by the South African Police. It was not until the late 1990s that the Dutch Reformed Church of South Africa finally apologized to him.

When we met with Beyers one sunny afternoon, he was in his early eighties, frail and beautiful and almost translucent, with the shining eyes of a seer. I asked him what had kept him going all these years, when everything seemed so hopeless or in check.

He replied that it was "the beauty of the Black South African soul, the uncanny ability of Black South Africans to forgive, their unwillingness to call for vengeance under the lash of so much terrible suffering." And he traced this to the African value called *Ubuntu.*

In the long traditions of African tribal society, *Ubuntu* means that no one is ever fully human except in communion with other human beings. When I asked whether this was a value brought to South Africa by Christian missionaries, Beyers thought carefully and said: "No, it is an ancient pre-Christian value deep in the African soul, a priceless gift that Africans have to teach us Christians, if only we could hear."

Under Mandela's charismatic leadership from 1994 to 1999, and under the subsequent two-term leadership of President Thabo Mbeki, and now under Jacob Zuma, the New South Africa has been committed to a way of

national reconciliation and healing that has been sim
ply awesome, given the road of vengeful retribution that
might have easily been taken by the black majority then
very powerful. Jacob Zuma and his ANC government are
showing less than shining leadership right now, and the
mood in the country is dark and restless. But the awesome call to reconciliation goes on beneath it all.

Speaking of the New South Africa, Alistair Sparks,
one of the most perceptive observers on the scene, commented while we were there: "What a stunning irony
this present prospect represents, of the symbol of racism
becoming the broker of a new cooperative relationship
between the white and dark-skinned nations of the world,
and the polecat of the world becoming a major new force
in international affairs."

In the vibrant midst of all its shining political and
social visions, South Africa is an awesomely beautiful
country, with sweeping coastlines along the Indian and
Atlantic Ocean and the spectacular Table Mountain
rising above the gorgeous city of Cape Town. The whole
grandeur of the country somehow flashed before us when
we one day visited a magnificent Wildlife Park in the
Transkei, where we thrilled to see springboks, reeboks,
warthogs, a curl-horned antelope, impalas, zebras, then
three giraffes and four white rhinos together at a water
hole. I was breathless at the silent beauty of it all, and I
remember it fondly to this day.

The vision of a non-racial democracy speaks as much
to us Americans as it does to South Africans. "Ah, but
your land is beautiful!" was the distracted murmur that

Alan Paton kept hearing from white visitors passing through South Africa. It is easy for us whites to live in a "normal" way here in the United States, as if we were not in the midst of a national crisis of interracial misery, injustice and violence. Of course, it is always in the back of our minds, and we even get better all the time at describing it.

But even today, in my quieter moments, I sometimes ask myself, "What in the world does South Africa have to teach us?" Warts and all, I still find it the most interesting and exciting country in the whole world. I really have left my heart there, and I would go back any time.

And all of this comes home even more forcefully right now as the world mourns the passing of its great architect, Nelson Mandela, *Madiba*, in his 95th year. He was a great hero, and the most dynamic and beloved world leader of our time. His shining work deeply informed the civil rights movement here in the United States, and his call for reconciliation between the races is still ringing clearly in the continuing struggles of South Africa and around the world.

I remember so well watching Nelson Mandela receive final word of his election as the first post-apartheid President, and hearing his gentle affirmation that "South Africa is a Rainbow People at peace with itself and with the world." Praise the Lord for the great blessing that Madiba was, and may we all be somehow worthy of it.

Zambia and Zimbabwe

In 1994, while still in Cape Town, we also stretched our wings into more of Southern Africa, with a week in Zambia and a week in Zimbabwe. Zambia is the former British colony of Northern Rhodesia, once with a thriving copper economy and rich, fertile land. Then, nearly thirty years into independence, a plethora of plagues—like endless drought, a collapsed copper market, and incompetent corrupt politicians—ravaged the country and its people.

And the terrible poverty was compounded by the Economic Structural Adjustment Policies, or ESAPs, that went with loans from the International Monetary Fund and the World Bank, so it was not hard to wonder how Zambia was ever going to survive.

We were hosted by an old Jesuit friend from Oregon, Peter Henriot, and, to our very great pleasure, we were also warmly received by the community of Jesuits wherever we went. Peter directed a thriving Theological Reflection Center in Lusaka, the capital city. He had travelled widely through central and southern Africa since he had come to Zambia four years earlier, so we appreciated his sharp political and social analysis of the broader African scene.

Two other American priest friends, whom we discovered teaching in the seminary in Lusaka, arranged for us to stay for some days in a guest house at the seminary. That gave us a chance to meet some of the young Africans who were coming into leadership in the Zambian church. They were a very striking group as they filed into chapel in their long white cassocks, even if their stolid liturgy and their rather formal seminary routine seemed to us pretty conventional and still very Western.

That was distinctly not the case when Peter took us to his very African mission church in the countryside. As their honored guests, two chairs were set up for us under a tree outside the simple building; and each of the villagers, elders down to the smallest children, came and shook our hands, in silence and with great courtesy, as they passed in to Mass.

The liturgy was clearly African and clearly their own, and it rocked with drums and dance and ululating and singing with their whole bodies and whole voices. We were totally caught up in the infectious wonder of it all. At one point, the lay leader of the parish introduced us, and everyone came forward singing and dancing to shake our hands again, and they dropped a small coin in a plate as a gift to us. We diplomatically asked later if the gift could go for something in the parish; and at the end, we each gave a little speech, and everyone danced back out into the sunshine.

But the real high point of our Zambia week was our visit to Victoria Falls. It was an eight-hour drive south from Lusaka through brown and barren farmlands, over a main highway that was so deeply pot-holed and rutted that you couldn't go more than 30 mph. I was glad I did not have to drive and thread my way through that torturous trail. And then, at the Zimbabwe border, the Zambezi River, which is called Southern Africa's "River of Life," opens up into the magnificent wonder that is Victoria Falls.

We found it far more majestic than Niagara, and we spent a whole day there, walking the long rim on both the Zim and the Zam sides of the canyon. The Zambezi is Africa's fourth largest river system. While we stood on its banks, the roaring river flow was not too much, but just enough to raise enormous clouds of roiling white mist, creating a dripping rain-forest over us at some points, and then clearing into magical rainbows in the afternoon sun. An awesome experience, which we never quite captured on the whole roll of film we shot that wonderful day.

We then flew on to Harare, the capitol of Zimbabwe, where we were met by our hosts, John and Kathy Stewart. John, who is a nephew of our friend, Anne Hope, was the Southern Africa staff person for the American Friends Service Committee, and Kathy was coordinating a remarkably innovative and effective education program for rural women.

Doris Lessing's *African Laughter* describes how she travelled with Kathy Stewart and her team throughout Zimbabwe in a Paolo Freire-based project called Community Publishing Process, where several thousand rural women were each actively involved in the writing of a book on their own development. It is a very exciting story, and we were delighted to hear about it from Kathy and her friends.

Until 1980, Zimbabwe was the British colony of Southern Rhodesia, and Harare was the crown jewel city of Salisbury. Today, it is a gleaming modern metropolis where most things seem to work most of the time, and the countryside appeared green and flourishing—the very antithesis of the crumbling infrastructure and dusty poverty of Lusaka and rural Zambia, the other Rhodesia to the north.

John and Kathy arranged lodging with a very hospitable woman friend and put us in touch with a wide range of church, human rights and public interest law groups, so that we spent lots of good time talking day and night on all sorts of issues.

Among the many critical opinions we heard of the Mugabe government, one theme kept coming back, just as it had in Zambia: the ESAPs of the World Bank were creating untold suffering for the poor in Zimbabwe.

This point was made with special force at Silveira House, a large and very creative training and education center for rural development outside Harare. It had been founded by the Jesuits and was now run almost entirely by Africans from the surrounding Shona villages.

Silveira House published an excellent series of concise popular studies on the impact of structural adjustment policies on health and nutrition, education, the cost of living, land access, and the living conditions of farm worker families. Their facts about ESAPs were drawn from extensive surveys of real people in the villages and cities, and their economic, social and theological analysis was very valuable and being widely used.

From Harare, we drove south for three days to Bulawayo, stopping off to see the ruins of the Great

Zimbabwe, a fascinating walled village and hillside fortress that goes back a thousand years. They are reputed to be the most extensive and best preserved archeological ruins in all of Africa. It is a near Wonder of the World, and marvelous shapes and shadows kept emerging as the sun moved through our whole day there.

Our visits to these neighboring countries, all of which have passed through liberation struggles into a shaky independence, helped us to see South Africa in a deeper focus, as if we were peering through the looking-glass out to where South Africa would also someday find itself in the coming years. To be sure, South Africa had a lot more going for it than most other African nations, and we believed that South Africa's political and social transition would succeed as few others had.

But it was clear to us that the overriding question for South Africa, as this second phase of their liberation was beginning, was whether enough change could be produced quickly enough to meet the legitimate expectations of the eighty-five percent of the population that was black. Peace and political stability were far more rooted than they were in the bad old days of apartheid, but they were still very fragile and tenuous.

A government of national unity in South Africa was a remarkable instrument for working through a five-year transition period by political consensus rather than by raw revolutionary demands. But creating new democratic processes at the local level was going very slowly, and it was obvious that whites who were still in power were putting off making the hard decisions as long as possible.

The white pro-apartheid right had evaporated as a threatening force. If all hell would break loose, it would now come not from whites but from impatient blacks. Somehow the political struggles which we saw in Zambia and Zimbabwe brought all of that South African turmoil into fresh new light for us.

When we came home from Southern Africa and settled down in San Francisco in 1994, I had cataract surgery and received a fresh new lens in my left eye. I also had a total replacement of my right hip. As I got in touch with this new cadmium and plastic hip, I began to realize that I was almost an Elder now.

But the real test for the new hip was when, three months into recovery, Donna and I went with an Elderhostel group for two weeks in Assisi. With me still limping quite a bit, we walked the medieval cobble-stoned hill towns of Umbria and Tuscany, ending up with several days in Florence, with its magnificent Duomo and its Campanile, crafted so magnificently by Giotto. The sight of those two still thrills me to this day.

It was really a grand experience, and we can't recommend Elderhostel too highly. Don't be put off by the "elder" part, by the way. It just means anyone 55 and over, and they put you into as many private homes as possible on your trip. Our small group was a remarkably vital and interesting crowd, and we corresponded with a few of them for some time thereafter.

In October of 1995, I was invited to go to Pasadena for several months as Interim Director of the regional office of the AFSC. That spiritual "leading," as the

Quakers would call it, felt just right with me, since I
had long admired the Service Committee's work and its
non-violent justice commitments, and I had very much
enjoyed my earlier service as an Interim Director in San
Francisco in 1991, and again in Atlanta in 1992.

I had a staff of thirty with exciting projects in Southern California, New Mexico, Arizona and Hawaii. I
insisted on a travel budget to fly home every weekend
to be with Donna, saying that yes, a split-level marriage
is manageable, but life is short. So I had a little studio
apartment in Pasadena, a borrowed VW Bug, and I
joined the commuter crowd from Burbank to San Francisco every weekend. I was there into May, until the new
Director came. Again, it was really good work.

Pilgrims in Pilgrim Place

And then began a whole new chapter in our search
for community on the pilgrim journey. While I still had
some final AFSC commitments in Pasadena, in April of
1996 we sold our house in San Francisco and moved to
Pilgrim Place in Claremont.

Pilgrim Place is a marvelous ecumenical retirement
community of 330 church professionals and activists from
sixteen denominations, founded by the Congregational
Church in 1915. Donna and I were only the third and
fourth Roman Catholics ever to come, and it took a little
while to settle into the new mix of ecclesiastical voices.

Pilgrim Place is a politically dynamic community
of people who have worked in social justice projects in

many countries around the world, and you don't see many rocking chairs on front porches around here. We have recently welcomed a married couple of Buddhist women, and as a community we are a diverse and spiritually committed people who really care about each other, care for each other, and care deeply for the world. Our greatest challenge is to choose among the vast variety of options that are always before us.

Wonderful things also happen on the campuses of the Claremont Colleges just across town. Some six colleges and a school of Theology offer speakers and music and cultural events of enticing proportions, and that makes for lots of interesting things always going on to keep us "retired" folks busy.

In my first few years here, I spent a fair amount of time in what I can only call priestly pastoral service as a Chaplain in our Health Services Center. I just try to be my priestly person, and being recognized as priest in a whole new way feeds me deeply. I feel truly lifted up and nourished by all those around me, and we are continually moved by the marvelous reality of interdependence that binds us all together. Pilgrim Place is for Donna and me truly The Beloved Community, an incredible gift of the Spirit at this point in our lives.

In April of 1996, as we were planning for our move to Claremont, we also came to Ed Bacon to talk to him about becoming members of All Saints Episcopal Church, about 40 miles away in Pasadena. I had often been invited to speak at All Saints, and Ed had recently become the dynamic Rector there, following on the great leadership of George Regas.

I remember so well sitting across Ed's desk facing a large and famous Rubens portrait of Ignatius Loyola in his classic fiddle-back vestments, and when he told me that he makes an eight-day Ignatian retreat every year, I thought the Spirit must be saying something special to me here.

We told Ed Bacon that by becoming members of All Saints we were not becoming Anglicans, but we were rather declaring ourselves to be "Transdenominational Christians with Roots in the Roman Catholic Tradition." And that seemed fine all around.

All Saints is the finest local church we have ever found in all the world, and I come away each week feeling nourished deeply by the Word and the Table and the vibrant singing of this liturgically and politically vital Community. Praise the Lord for such a gift, and may we somehow be worthy of it.

I go to All Saints every Sunday primarily to gather with the Christian community around the table of the Lord, around the Eucharistic table. And here is where my deep commitment to liturgical sign drives me. Ecumenism is not simply reconciling doctrinal differences between Christians. It is rather being together in common action for the poor and the hungry and all those who need peace and reconciliation in the world.

I simply must come to the communion table in order to share with the rest of the believing community in what Jesus called his *"Body-to-be-broken"* and his *"Blood-to-be-poured-out"* for the world. I am called to commune with that Christ, to make myself one with Him who has broken his body and poured out his blood for me and for all the world.

"*Accompaniment*" is a richly symbolic term for me. It means to "break bread with," and that term and "*compassion*," which means to "suffer with," are compelling values that richly feed me.

Both of these visions have been driving forces in my work for justice and social change—not just sharing in the pain and the sorrow, but also sharing in the joys of the whole world of those to whose service I have been called. I am not just an organizer, but I am an organizer with a vision, a vision of transforming the world through the power and presence of the broken and redeeming Christ in that world, whose body and whose hands we are.

Slowly Settling In

For a long time after moving here to our spacious and wonderful three-bedroom house at 737 Alden Road, a rather large addition to Pitzer Lodge, Pilgrim Place's Assisted Living unit, was under bustling construction just outside our window and all around us. The chronic noise and dust of it all prompted us to get out of town every chance we could, so for a long time we were on the road quite a bit.

In 1996, near the end of our first year on Alden Road, we spent a wonderful three weeks in Australia and New Zealand, prompted by our having very old frequent-flier miles on United that we had to either use or lose. Such are the deadlines that come with retirement!

In Sydney and Melbourne, we stayed at Grail centers, where the hospitality was just marvelous, and we gave talks at each place on "Growing Older," eliciting great interest in our Pilgrim Place experience. A highpoint for us was once standing by ourselves on a golf course fairway outside Melbourne at dusk, right in the center of about fifty wild kangaroos who suddenly silently gathered about us, one mama with her "joey" popping in and out of her pouch. Just wonderful.

In Cairns, near the Great Barrier Reef, we were received by a marvelous Grail member and her family. I fell in love with their little five-year old daughter, Monique, who, dressed in perky baseball cap and little backpack, led us briskly through a tropical botanical garden and excitedly told us the name of each of the exotic trees and flowers she dragged us along to. We also visited the mysterious Ayers Rock, now known as Uluru, its aboriginal name, and Alice Springs, and then we sailed silently across the magnificent Milford Sound in New Zealand.

In the summer of 1997, we did a marvelous three-week Elderhostel in Central Europe: a week each in Warsaw, Prague and Budapest. From my Innsbruck days as a student, I had always been drawn to and curious about Eastern Europe but had never quite gotten beyond Vienna, which I had loved dearly, and it was very satisfying to be back in that part of the world, even if only briefly.

We were just by ourselves, and we had a very stimulating look at three diverse national transitions to a "free" market economy, after the repressive boredom of fifty long years of Communist planning. The Jewish community and the Holocaust were overriding shadows in each country, and we made especially powerful visits to the Warsaw Ghetto and to Auschwitz-Birkenau, the extermination camp which was the largest killing center in the entire Nazi universe, later called "the very heart of their system." The grim and frozen stillness of the place is today simply awesome and frightening.

Then, a five-week European circuit in April and May of 1998 started with a fascinating Elderhostel in Sicily. We never knew how much history and magnificent art could be found on that neglected little island. Everyone who ever sailed through the Mediterranean bumped into Sicily and stayed awhile: Phoenicians, Greeks, Romans, Carthaginians, Byzantines, Arabs, Normans, Spaniards, Garibaldi and the new Italians, then Mussolini's Fascisti and finally the Mafiosi.

They left behind marvelous temples and frescoes and mosaics of awesome beauty, as well as traces of their politics, food, dress and dance that are still very alive in Sicilian culture today. That Elderhostel program in Sicily is really excellent, and we highly recommend it.

In 1998, we got a new Executive Director at Pilgrim Place, Bill Cunitz, a former Vice President at Andover Newton Theological School in Massachusetts, and I was both honored and delighted to serve on the Search Committee that called him. It was a very satisfying, Spirit-filled process; and Bill brought a vibrant new vision to us, as well as superb executive skills.

He listens carefully to all of us, and it is a real joy for me to feel I am part of such a well-run and supportive community. In fact, it is in no small part thanks to Bill Cunitz' dynamic leadership that today we have a waiting list of well more than a hundred persons to come to Pilgrim Place.

The latter part of 1998 got centered around some atrial fibrillation in my heart, which led to some angioplasty by a wonderful Indian cardiologist. The stainless steel stent which I now carry in my artery, which by chance had been found to be 90% blocked, and the titanium ball which I now carry in two replaced hip joints, as well as the plastic lens replacements in both my eyes, and more recently the insertion of a pacemaker on my heart, make me a candidate for Bionic Man of the Year, but I'm grateful to be bounding about in blessedly very good health even today.

Valuable Places To Be

In the summer of 1999, I found myself recovering from a left hip replacement, to balance the new right hip I had gotten six years earlier. Donna was again a marvelous caregiver, and I just kept moving on, even though it took longer to get my strength back this time.

But just then, the great new movement called "Jubilee 2000" was born. My new valuable place to be suddenly became obvious, and I got better in a hurry. The cancellation of unpayable Third World debt took over all my recovering energy, and it has remained a passion of mine

ever since. I went to Washington in April of 2000 for a
large J2K Mobilization on the Mall, even though I was
still limping around in pain by then. We encircled the
Capitol with a human chain of ten thousand people, and
I joined a thousand people on the Hill to lobby Congress
the next day.

I was glad to get back to my old haunts at Georgetown and around Washington, and the Mobilization was
an exciting and tonic event, full of energy and hope all
around. All that work finally paid off in November of
2000 with congressional passage of $435 million toward
cancelling the bilateral debt of thirty-one countries to the
U.S. That was good work then, and the Jubilee call for
debt cancellation continues to be heard today.

I still continued on my old circuit of burning issues,
searching for what might be the next valuable place for
me to be, at home or on the road. In 2003, I became particularly upset with what the U.S. was doing in Iraq, and
I put together a speaking tour around the country.

My talk was entitled, *"What if We Bring the Troops
Home, Now?"* And simply by word of mouth and email
flyers from my desk, I arranged to speak 43 times in ten
months around the country at schools and churches and
civic groups, on what to do about Iraq and how to get the
troops home now.

I'm still somewhat breathless thinking about how
I could have done all that without any staff or office
around me, but I was really consumed by Iraq. True,
we didn't quite "bring them home now," but it was very
exciting and good work, deeply satisfying.

Iraq is, of course, still with us, as well as Afghanistan, and all of this was painfully brought home to me recently by a *Los Angeles Times* article headed "America's Nation-Building at Gunpoint." A retired army Colonel pointed out that during the American occupation of Iraq, as many as 250,000 Iraqis died and 1.4 million were displaced. Nearly five thousand members of the American military were killed, with many thousands more suffering life-altering wounds, both physical and mental.

In Afghanistan, another two thousand Americans have been killed, with many more seriously wounded, along with thousands of Afghan civilians. In our totally misguided nation-building efforts, it is estimated that the United States has spent about $3 trillion in Iraq and close to $1 trillion in Afghanistan. A recent book by Joseph Stiglitz and Linda Bilmes is called *The Three Trillion Dollar War: The True Cost of the Iraq Conflict.* I can hardly bear to read it.

These horrendous figures are all really hard to absorb, and as a country we tend to simply turn away from them, even if we do happen to see them by chance in the haze of our controlled media. But they emphasize that the wars in Iraq and in Afghanistan have been terribly costly and terribly wrong.

My Magic Words

I have for many years been fed by the wonderful mantra, "It's going to be all right." I recall reaching for it in one of my earlier rounds as a Chaplain in our Health

Center here at Pilgrim Place.

Phoebe Anderson, a very bright and wonderfully frail old woman now gone to her reward, was sitting in the hall one day, fretting and picking nervously at her sweater, upset about all manner of things. "Oh, I'm a mess, I'm just a mess," she kept saying. When I told her she was not a mess, she shouted, "How do you know I'm not a mess?" Drawing back a bit, I said, "You're not a mess, Phoebe, because God made you, and God doesn't make messes."

I told her not to worry and that the magic words are: "It's going to be all right," and after looking hard at me, she quieted down gently. I felt pastorally content, and said I would quiz her on the magic words when I next came.

Then she suddenly turned on me and again shouted: "Just what is this 'it' that's going to be all right? Is it everything that's going to be all right?" After a quick back-pedal, and saying that this was indeed a profound theological question, I responded: "Yes, Phoebe, everything that the good Lord sends you will be all right. Yes, everything. Talk to your husband, Phil. He's a really good theologian, and maybe he can help you with what I mean."

I find it remarkable that echoes from this encounter continue to bounce off the walls of Pilgrim Place, people spontaneously recalling the phrase to me again and again. For several years, every time I came down the hall at the Health Center, Phoebe would shout out, "Here he comes, everybody. It's going to be all right!"

I'm honored that Willard Hunter, one of our Pilgrim Place greats, once called it my "mantra." That was high praise, but I really owed the community some history of the phrase. So I wrote a little piece, saying that I first came across it in the early 1970s in a very provocative little book by Peter Berger, *A Rumor of Angels: Modern Society and the Rediscovery of the Supernatural.*

A good Lutheran and a very fine sociologist, Peter Berger was reflecting on what he called "signals of transcendence," suggesting that there are "prototypical human gestures that may constitute such signals." In a wonderful image, Berger described one such signal, one such "rumor of angels."

A young child, he says, wakes up in the night from a bad dream, alone and surrounded by the darkness and nameless threats, instinctively calling for mother. Mother takes and cradles the child in the timeless gesture of the Magna Mater. She turns on a warm and reassuring lamp, rocks the child and softly says; "Don't be afraid, my dear, it's going to be all right."

How does the mother know that it's going to be all right, Berger asks. Is she lying to the child? And his response is no, because, willy-nilly, the role which parents take on "represents not only the order of this or that society, but order as such, the underlying order of the universe that it makes sense to trust." Whether or not she is aware of it, the reassuring mother is instinctively affirming that everything is indeed in order, everything is indeed all right.

This basic formula can be translated into a statement of cosmic scope: Have trust in being; being is ultimately favorable to us humans. I have preached this wonderful insight of Berger many times, and it rings in my soul often as I walk the quiet halls of this remarkable community called Pilgrim Place.

Our Festival

Our major event every year is our Pilgrim Place Festival in November, which commonly draws about ten thousand people to our campus from all over California and neighboring states. Most of those who come for the two days know that it is to support the residents of Pilgrim Place who have depleted their assets, and to somehow recognize their long years of service in the world.

We also welcome about a thousand persons who volunteer to help in our Food Court and at the various booths which sell artistic creations of many kinds made by Pilgrim residents, including weavings and beautiful paintings and stained-glass creations and toys and figures from our talented wood-workers.

I have immensely enjoyed the privilege of handing out colored balloons on long strings to make little children, and their smiling mothers, happy in the throngs. I had a troop of young Girl Scouts who made sure the balloons were tied tightly to the wrists of the jumping little ones to prevent the disaster of their blowing away.

I'm told that the price of helium has now gone so high that we're not going to have balloons anymore. That's a terrible shame, and life at the Festival will be less exciting without them.

I also look forward every year to my work at a booth called "Glue-In." Children get a square of cardboard and some flour-and-water paste, and they create proud little masterpieces out of chips of metal and plastic and wood from the carpenter shop, flotsam from our attics and attics around the city, and pieces of twigs and leaves from the trees on our wonderful campus.

All of this stands piled high in loaded wheelbarrows, and the kids pick through them frantically and then sit down at long tables to create their really quite awesome works of art. I sit outside and take their tickets, dressed in my broad-rimmed Pilgrim hat and black-and-white costume, and as the children come to me I have a little round stamp that only says "OK" on it.

I ask the kids to show me the back of their hand and tell me their name. So this nervous little one tells me her name is Jennifer. From under my big black hat, I look Jennifer right in the eye, and I say, "Jennifer, I have something very important to tell you." She is wide-eyed and expectant. I then stamp the back of her hand with my little round stamp that just says "OK" on it, and I say, "Jennifer, *you are OK, and don't ever let anyone tell you that you're not.*" As she jumps away, I also tell Mom that I think she's OK, too, and everyone is happy.

Once, I also told little five-year old Andrew that he was OK. As he went bouncing off to Glue-In, his mother told me that I had told Andrew that last year, too, and she wanted me to know that when Andrew came home last year I had changed his life.

Telling Jennifer "... you are OK," at Pilgrim Place Festival, 2013

He was a new little boy, she said. As he stood there in the kitchen, his shoulders were back and he was quiet and centered, and he kept saying, "He told me I am OK." The moment of her telling me that is still enough to keep me going for years to come. It was a wonderful experience. I take it to be a liturgical blessing, and I look forward to it all year with great delight.

I once had another experience with a little boy which is also still with me in happy memory. We have a large and colorful wooden ship called the Mayflower, on its way to Plymouth Landing. It is built up over a long truck and slowly takes children through the festival crowds.

With great flapping sails and about forty kids huddled around the Captain on its decks, it goes around with a loud honk-honk for all to get out of the way. One day, as I was giving out balloons, the Mayflower was about to come honking around the corner and stop in front of us to pick up more children.

In front of me I saw a marvelous little boy, maybe five years old, shouting wildly "It's coming! It's coming!" He was really ecstatic and jumping all about. And then he ran up to me and jumped right into my arms, shouting wildly in my face "It's coming!" I was so delighted that I thought I must use this in my Christmas preaching, and it has stayed with me ever since. The Lord is coming, and it's going to be all right.

More Good Work

Starting in 1996, I have been deeply involved with the Claremont Consultation, now called Progressive Christians Uniting. It had been founded in 1994 by theologian John Cobb and George Regas, the retired Rector of All Saints Church in Pasadena. I was on its Board of Directors for several years until not long ago.

Bringing together several denominations, PCU works dynamically on all sorts of organizing and social justice issues up and down the West Coast. For ten years it has been led by Peter Laarman, an ordained UCC minister who had served with distinction for many years as Senior Minister at Judson Memorial Church, on Washington Square in Lower Manhattan.

A splendid high point of 1998 was bringing Donna with me to a reunion of former Jesuits, at the Novitiate in

Wernersville, Pennsylvania, where I had first entered the Society of Jesus fifty-one years earlier. Thirty-five of us who had entered together came, along with ten spouses, and we spent three days sharing stories of our spiritual journeys—some of us, like me, not having been in touch for more than thirty years.

It was wonderful to walk those long marble halls with Donna, and have her sleep near me on single beds in a simple 4'x10' open room like the one I silently lived in for four years. Of all the Jesuits who entered after 1947, my first year, 68% have now left the order, almost three to one. Ignatian spirituality is clearly still our bond, so we need to think in new ways about who's in and who's out. And that's a challenge that I sometimes turn about in my head. Jesuits, especially now with our new Jesuit Pope, Francis, are still very much a part of me.

Our most momentous event of 1999 was when a routine mammogram for Donna revealed some breast cancer. She had just returned from a glorious Elderhostel week in London, going to the theater with her sister, Paula. After lots of research and discussion, Donna decided to have a bilateral mastectomy, and the surgery went well, with no need for follow-up radiation or chemotherapy.

She recovered rather quickly, no doubt thanks to all the prayers and healing energies which so many people sent her way. Within five weeks, she began teaching a course for community people on Legal Issues for the Elderly, three hours at a stretch on her feet. I call her my "most beautiful Twiggy in all the world," and I'm constantly in awe at the spiritual strength and energy she brings to whatever comes her way.

As I mentioned earlier, I served regularly for several months as Chaplain in our Health Center here, and I still look forward today to that moving experience of being brought deeper into the adventure of touching and hugging and strengthening one another in the mysterious passages from gradual diminishment into promising new life. It is good to be an Elder, and I fervently hope that the best is yet to come.

Back to South Africa

By the end of summer in 1999, Donna had gathered good new strength, and we went ahead with a long-planned return to South Africa. As I've already recounted, we had spent two exciting years in Cape Town in 1993-94, sixteen months before the election of Nelson Mandela and seven months after. We decided it was time to go back and see how our friends had experienced the first five years of the new South Africa, and how they were seeing the newly elected president, Thabo Mbeki.

So, after a week's stop-over with Scottish and English friends in Ayr and Oxford, we went on to three wonderful weeks in Cape Town, staying right on the coast with Nancy Gordon, dear friend and recent widow of Gerald Gordon, a renowned novelist who had also been a leading human rights attorney in the Apartheid era. No tourism on this return trip, just meeting and eating with friends Black, Colored, Indian and White.

We went out to Robben Island, and had a moving

visit to the tiny cell where Nelson Mandela spent most of
his 27 years in prison. It was a delight to attend the dedi-
cation of a wonderful new Grail retreat and conference
center in Kleinmond, just outside Cape Town, on the
edge of a mountain reserve and a short walk to a lovely
curving beach on the Indian Ocean.

We hadn't really planned it that way, so it was just ser-
endipity to be at that Grail center for their great occasion.
Donna was asked to give one of several blessings offered
in different languages, and she began planning with
them for an international conference on Growing Older
in the Grail, which took place at Kleinmond in 2000.

That brought together forty-five Grail members from
ten countries, and Donna came back to be among them.
It was marvelous that older women from such diverse
backgrounds could come together to share common concerns about leaving fulltime employment, health care,
growing older and dying well.

Of so many impressions from those brief three weeks
in Cape Town, a few things were especially remarkable.
The cycle of exhilaration was certainly over. After five
years of Nelson Mandela's charismatic, healing leadership, Thabo Mbeki was bringing new energy and serious-
ness to the challenge of economic renewal.

We found Mbeki's economic program more conservative than we had expected, geared above all to foreign
investment and export trade, with touches that almost
sounded like the bad old Structural Adjustment policies
of the World Bank, without much attention to the needs
of the poor. After being isolated for so long, the era of

economic globalization had become real to them for the
first time. And the visions of a shining Rainbow Nation
were under great strain, as is even truer today.

Again To China

In August of 2001, I was invited to return as Interim
Regional Director for the American Friends Service
Committee for five months in San Francisco, so we
rented an apartment three blocks from our old co-op
apartment of nineteen years on Ellis Street.

The AFSC had grown, and this time, I had a staff of
thirty-two, a budget of $1.8 million, urban and rural or-
ganizing programs in six Northern California locations,
some very difficult personnel problems, and a challenge
to search nationally for a new Regional Director. It was
a lot of work for such a short few months, and a good
part of its stress also came from the terrible events of 9-11
which were suddenly echoing all around us.

Our major foreign adventure of that year was a long-
planned three-week return trip to China in October,
which I took with Donna while on leave from the AFSC.
We were a small group of seventeen, led by good friends
Jean and Franklin Woo. Jean was born in China, Frank
in San Francisco Chinatown. Both had long served in
Hong Kong and then were for many years the China
Desk at the National Council of Churches in New York,
regularly leading study tours to China.

We were received everywhere by officers of the China
Christian Council and the government Religious Affairs

Bureau, and our focus on the complexities of religious life made an interesting entry point for us into contemporary China.

We went to a pre-Vatican II Mass in Latin in a small parish church, and we had a wonderful tour of the graves of Matteo Ricci and the other early Jesuit missionaries in China. From my earliest Jesuit years, Matteo Ricci had been a legendary hero of mine, so it was a moving, special pilgrimage for me to kneel at his gravesite, situated within a training center for bureaucratic officials of the Chinese Communist Party.

We had, of course, been to China sixteen years earlier, as guests of the Chinese government, on a very exciting ten-person "peace delegation." The development of every level of Chinese life in the sixteen years since that visit was simply beyond description. China was indeed a great sleeping giant coming alive, as Mao had famously said back in 1949.

I was continually in awe at the size of it all—1.3 billion people, almost a quarter of the whole human race, organized into a single political, economic and social unit. It was about four times the size of the U.S. population, in roughly the same geographical area, but they had only about 11% of the country's arable land on which to feed their more than a billion people.

Beijing and Shanghai were now shining showcases of free-market capitalism, with all its blessings and its downsides. Unfortunately, once again, where there used to be bicycles and rickshaws there were now cars, trucks and buses, with disastrous consequences to air quality and traffic congestion in all the major cities.

We spent four fine days cruising down the Long River ("Yangzte") through the dazzling Three Gorges to the site of the world's biggest dam, which was rushing towards completion in the following year. It would displace some 1.3 million peasants who would need to move to higher ground as the gorges filled. The vast size of this whole landscape was simply awesome.

Our hearts and minds were warmed by our visit to a remote mountaintop village of Miao Christians in Yunnan Province, among the largest of the fifty-six ethnic minority groups in China.

Our bus slowly climbed to about ten thousand feet on a narrow dirt track, and we were greeted with cheers by seventy young choir members in native costume, some of whom had walked six hours to come to sing for us in heavenly and very sophisticated four-part harmony. It was all a very memorable experience, and I would go back anytime.

I was doing a lot of work on globalization and world trade issues at the time, and particularly on NAFTA and the Free Trade Area of the Americas, so I kept talking globalization and economic issues all over China.

I had just given a talk in Monterey on these issues, and I was delighted to be invited to give that paper to about two hundred theological faculty and students in Nanjing, with special reference to what I thought would be the impact of China's coming entry into the World Trade Organization.

I was really impressed that they seemed to understand my English, and I got a very warm and informed reaction. I later sent the paper to four of those folks, with hopes of staying in contact as they felt the bite of the WTO into their markets. That never quite happened, but China still has a very warm place in my heart.

Near Christmas in 2001, in what turned into a marvelous little adventure, we set up an AFSC project in San Francisco to receive blankets in good condition for Afghan refugees. We would get them from local churches and Friends Meetings and store them in some garages nearby, and the idea caught on incredibly well.

We packed up the blankets in large fresh boxes and shipped them to Philadelphia by huge trailer, and from there by ship—with a guaranteed route that the blankets would really get to AFSC personnel in the refugee camps, in good time for Christmas.

One day, we had forty adults and kids in the Friends Meeting House and our office on Market Street, and we finally loaded three trailers, with great energy and spirit. All of this with lots of TV and print coverage for Christmas, and I can still feel the energy.

The following day, a mother proudly came by with four brand new wool blankets from K-Mart, saying that all her children had agreed that they would send these blankets to the refugee children instead of getting Christmas presents that year. It was very moving for me to hear her, another wonderful step on my continuing Quaker journey.

Grieving Time

We found it very difficult to be painfully apart for those long months from the community we had grown so to love at Pilgrim Place, and we grieved the deaths of a number of close friends within a six-week period late that summer.

In 2001, we mourned especially the loss of Mary Louise Tully, an honored very early American Grail member with whom Donna had lived and worked in Amsterdam many years earlier. Then there was Rose Marciano Lucey, who had been a founder of the Christian Family Movement with her husband, Dan, and all her life an ardent worker for peace and justice around the world.

And, most painful of all, we lost Robert McAfee Brown, one of the dearest and greatest of the giants for justice in our time and one of the closest friends and compañeros with whom we have been blessed in our lives.

And the next year was also a time of deep grieving for us, with the death of two very dear and wonderful friends here at Pilgrim Place, Pat Reif and Victoria Jadez. Pat had been a member of the Immaculate Heart Community, a valiant group of courageous women who had rejected the benighted tyranny of James Cardinal McIntyre of Los Angeles after Vatican II, in order to live out their call to the renewal of religious life in a fresh new Catholic tradition.

Pat was a fine ecumenical and feminist theologian, an inspiring and insightful teacher, a tenacious tennis player, and a dedicated activist on a remarkable range of social justice issues all her life. We had so very much in common, even though I never could have matched her on the tennis court.

In the last days around her bed, Pat and I designed a memorial service in which one of her closest IHM friends joined me in concelebrating what we called "A Transdenominational Celebration of the Lord's Supper, with Roots in the Roman Catholic Tradition."

More than three hundred of Pat's friends from all over Southern California, including many of her IHM sisters, gathered at Pilgrim Place for that remarkable event, which was followed by a warm reception.

The baker in Claremont Village donated specially baked breads for the Eucharist, because he had known and warmly admired Pat, and chalices from six denominations were offered by Pilgrim residents to serve the wine made holy. All of this was not at all common in those days, and it was the first time that the ecumenical community of Pilgrim Place had ever been together around an open Lord's Table.

The experience left lasting spiritual traces, and we still resonate to Pat's presence among us. She is still fondly remembered in the Pat Reif Memorial Lectures at the Claremont School of Theology.

Victoria Jadez was one of the most sensitive and beautiful spirits among us, a lifetime member of the Grail with Donna, and a dear friend to many of us. For many years she had brilliantly managed a retreat and conference center in Menlo Park, in the San Francisco Bay Area.

Pilgrims at Pilgrim Place, 2000

She met regularly with a Zen prayer group here, lived in warm and striking simplicity, and worked every week bringing food to the hungry in a Council of Churches project in Pomona.

Donna and I joined in a very moving group of Victoria's Pilgrim friends who sat regularly around her bed until the day she died. We helped her remember her remarkable life, talked at her request about the meaning of her dying, and warmly sent her on her way. We later drafted an account of our "Journeying With Victoria," which I still have, and it was Pilgrim Place at its best.

In spring, 2002, we spent several weeks in Britain, visiting friends in Oxford and attending a fascinating conference in North Wales, on a project created by our Anglican priest friend, Jim Cotter, called Small Pilgrimage Places. We went around to visit some of those pilgrim places in local parishes, and we found it a very exciting venture.

We also had several family reunions of the extended Ogren clan, Donna's family, one up on Monterey Bay and one at Christmas down in Mazatlan, Mexico. We then spent Thanksgiving with old friends in Honolulu, Simon and Lorraine Klevansky, tacking on a week to cruise several of the Hawaian Islands. Even with all this, we never quite used up our Frequent Flyer miles.

Middle East concerns continued to absorb a large part of my consciousness. I used to spend about an hour a day reading email from inside Israel and Palestine, but I finally found that I could no longer really handle knowing so much first-hand about the terrible injustice and pain in that all but hopeless struggle.

However, I came upon a singular ray of hope when we happened to hear a talk by an Orthodox Israeli Jew named Yitzak Frankenthal. His son, Arik Frankenthal, a nineteen-year old soldier in the Israeli army, had been kidnapped and killed by Hamas in 1994. The next year, Yitzak Frankenthal founded what he called "Parents Circle: Bereaved Families Supporting Reconciliation, Tolerance and Peace."

It brought together 450 Palestinian and Israeli Jewish families in Israel who had lost immediate family members due to the conflict. And, most imaginatively, it sponsored a program called "Hello-Shalom-Salaam," which provided translation and a phone link for thousands of Israelis and Palestinians who would just like to talk with someone "from the other side."

It cheered me to feel the hope around this brave man, and his pioneering work has evolved today into "The Parents Circle Families Forum," a grassroots Palestinian-Israeli organization of now over six hundred families around the world, all of whom have lost a family member as a result of the prolonged conflict. The Forum is supported by the "Fund for Reconciliation, Tolerance and Peace," and it builds on their conviction that a historic reconciliation between these two nations is a necessary condition for finding a sustainable peace.

One of their most imaginative projects has been to organize summer camps for bereaved Israeli and Palestinian kids. The Parents Circle is still very much alive today, and it reminds me of the Truth and Reconciliation Commission which we found so remarkable in South Africa. You can learn more at *www.theparentscircle.com.*

In 2002 Donna had been asked by some friends to run for the California Senior Legislature, in open ballot in Los Angeles County. CSL is a creation of state law, funded by contributions in a check-off on our state income tax form. Matching the State Legislature, there are 40 Senior Senators and 80 Senior Assembly Members, and it has a respected lobbying voice. I'm proud to say that Pilgrim Place packed the ballot box, and Donna was elected to it in June.

In October, I went with Donna to her first CSL meeting, held in the State Legislature's chambers in the Capitol in Sacramento. Donna was formally seated as a Senior Assembly Member, and I volunteered as a messenger, running between committees and the floor in the four-day meeting. It was very exciting to see my wife in this important position, getting state legislators to sponsor twenty bills which the SCL had voted as their top priorities. She was back and forth to Sacramento frequently in the next two years.

Another World Is Possible

2003 was a very full year. It began with a three-week trip to Brazil in January, leading a group of students from San Francisco State. My main purpose was to go with them to the World Social Forum in Porto Alegre. The World Social Forum had been set up three years earlier as a people's forum, a balance and an alternative to the World Economic Forum, where government and corporate wizards gather every year in glitzy chalets in Davos, Switzerland, to imperiously set the economic future of all of us from their snowy mountaintop, behind guarded doors.

Porto Alegre was the antithesis to that, and probably ten times larger than any conference I had ever attended. 100,000 (!) people came from 123 countries, to march and listen and talk together with an awesome racial and ethnic diversity that was just thrilling to be swallowed up in.

There were 1,300 roundtables, lectures, seminars and workshops in five different venues all across Porto Alegre, among which I could choose only a carefully selected few. The theme was "Another World is Possible," and that cry still resonates in my soul echoing from the languages of the meeting: Portuguese, Spanish, French and English.

The main focus was on sharing experiences and bonding together to transform the injustices of globalization and the Free Trade Area of the Americas. The terrible shadow of the Iraq war, along with the 800-pound gorilla called the New American Empire, hung over the discussions. People from around the world were sensitive and even supportive, but it was at times painful to be an American in that crowd.

The many international exchanges I had in those four days were blessedly tonic for me, and I came away with enormous new energy and hope. At the closing session, the Indian author and activist, Arundhati Roy, gently concluded with the statement:

> We are many, and they are few. They need us more than we need them. Another world is not only possible, she is on her way. And on a quiet day, if you really listen, you can hear her breathing.

Still today, I take that to be the creative Spirit of God breathing over the chaos of the void and the deep. "Another World is Possible." *"Un Otro Mundo es Posible!"*

Amen, I say, may it be. And let's get about it.

In the months after that, I gave about thirty talks on all these issues to church and community groups up and down California, with a special focus on "The National Security Strategy of the USA," the arrogant statement of George Bush in September 2002 which I still consider the most important, and terrifying, political document of the new era which it ushered in.

It aggressively and radically altered the history of U.S. foreign policy, declaring the New American Empire's unilateral right to preemptively attack anyone who might even dream of challenging our colossal military power. This is the policy and rhetoric of exceptionalism which is unfortunately still so much with us today.

About that time, Donna and I enjoyed a very full three days in Madison, Wisconsin, where a wonderful progressive Democratic group had invited me to speak four times around the university and also do two radio talk shows, with calls coming in from all over southern Wisconsin.

I have mentioned my being on the Board of Progressive Christians Uniting, a broad group of church folks which insists that not all Christians are politically conservative, especially on justice issues. PCU ran a two-day conference in June of 2003 in Pasadena, entitled (imagine!) "A Better World is Possible: Christian Faith and Economic Justice." I chaired the planning team, and four hundred people came.

Keynoters were my old friend, Walden Bello, from Bangkok, and Maude Barlow from Canada, and there were twenty splendid workshops. It came off very well, and some good organizing work resulted from it. I was glad to have spent almost six months of my life on it. In August, we went briefly to Joshua Trees National Park, quietly enriching our souls with wildflowers and splendid geological formations, and then on to Montana for an excellent Elderhostel in Yellowstone Park.

To top the year, Donna and I went to Ireland and then briefly to western Scotland for three weeks. For a long time we read nothing but the complex history and culture of Ireland, where we had never been, so our time there was especially enjoyable and rewarding. We rented a car in Dublin and drove all around the country for ten days, staying in B&Bs along the gorgeous coast. We ended up in Belfast, where we listened to Irish relatives and friends of our dear friend, Patricia McGinnis, as they recounted vivid, first-hand stories about The Troubles and their hopes for a peace settlement in the near future.

A major gift of that year was the chance I had to speak about Jonathan Schell's then new book, *The Unconquerable World: Power, Nonviolence, and the Will of the People.* Schell had always been a great hero of mine, and I spoke in many places on this great work, which I found to be the most lucid and provocative book I had read in twenty years.

I also remembered Schell's 1981 bestseller, *The Fate of the Earth,* on the threat of nuclear annihilation. He spoke once at All Saints in Pasadena, and Donna and I had a warm lunch with him afterwards. It was a great treat for me to unpack his enthusiasms about Gandhi and

Vaclav Havel and the splendor of non-violent power in the history of revolutions around the world.

I found Jonathan Schell's insights enormously helpful in my search for the valuable place to be in these dark days of American militarism, and I stayed in email contact with him for some time.

As somebody famous once said, "I've come to expect the worst, but it's always worse than I expected." That's me today, so I proposed a four-session seminar on Schell's ideas with Pilgrim Place residents. About fifty residents bought his book and together we tried to really listen, with a faith that we could hear the Spirit breathing over the void in new and hopeful ways.

My energies in 2004 were almost exclusively centered on the "National Security Strategy of the United States" and "The New American Empire," because I find this arrogantly aggressive policy so destructive of a peaceful future for all the peoples of the earth.

In ten months, I spoke to forty-six university, church and community groups around the country, with special invitations to the national convention of the Fellowship of Reconciliation in Pasadena and an international Peace Conference in British Columbia. I was often breathless with the excitement of it all.

It had all started with an email I sent far and wide, offering to speak to any group, for expenses only and without a stipend, as my contribution to regime change in Washington. Along the way, I realized that I was really doing peace education as well as political organizing, and that was very satisfying.

As I burrowed deeper into the Bush imperial policy and its awful consequences, I realized what a depressing trip I was laying on my audiences, and I wondered if I was becoming just shrill.

Bill Moyers, one of my most valued gurus, helped me right then when he said: "One of the biggest changes in politics in my lifetime is that the delusional is no longer marginal. It has come in from the fringe, to sit in the seats of power in the Oval Office and in Congress. And a challenge for us journalists is how to tell such a story without coming across as Cassandras, without turning off the people we most want to understand what's happening, who must act on what they read and hear."

Bill Moyers is anything but a Cassandra, and his welcome voice calmed my spirit. "The delusional is no longer marginal. It has come in from the fringe, to sit in the seats of power." I believe that, and I try to reach for every hopeful strand I can find, still telling the story as it is.

D-Day In Normandy

In May of 2004 Donna and I went to France for a river cruise on the Seine, and then some quiet time in Paris. We had our thrilling highpoint when we went first to Normandy for the sixtieth memorial of the D-Day landings on June 6, 1944. On the high bluff above Omaha Beach, scene of the bloodiest battle of all, we laid flowers on a grave in the American cemetery, where ten thousand (!) American soldiers lie under rows of silent white crosses and Stars of David.

And on June 6th itself, at the Peace Memorial in Caen, we witnessed an extraordinary ceremony of reconciliation between the leaders of France and Germany, Jacques Chirac and Gerhard Schroeder, solemnly standing face to face on a large open stage before thousands of people from many nations.

When Gerhard Schroeder gave a very powerful and emotional address, Jacques Chirac was deeply moved, warmly accepting the call for French reconciliation with the German people. With genuine warmth, Chirac said, "To those who confront one another in the endless night of hatred and resentment, our reconciliation offers a genuine hope. On this day of reconciliation and hope, French women and French men receive you more than ever as a friend. They receive you as a brother." The Frenchman then reached out and gave the German a great bear-hug, to popping flash-bulbs and the cheers of the many nations represented.

There was no playing to the balconies, just a brief and deeply sincere commitment by two dignified leaders, in the name of each of their peoples, that there shall never again be war between France and Germany. It was a class act, and the solemn power of it brought me to tears.

The event was of truly historic importance, an awesome spark of hope and possibility in an otherwise dark and desperate time, and I still vividly remember it. I wrote it all up in an article called "A New Europe at Normandy," which was published in the journal of the Fellowship of Reconciliation.

When we came home, we went up to La Casa de

Maria in Santa Barbara, for a retreat with Dan Berrigan. Dan has long been a dear friend and a great hero of mine, and I have always treasured his reflections on political and social justice issues, so it was wonderful to prayerfully ponder with him for a few days all that we had so warmly experienced at Normandy.

At that time, I had just finished reading *Sarge*, the provocative biography of the life and times of Sargent Shriver by Scott Tossel. It was good for the soul to revisit the heady days of the Peace Corps, the War on Poverty, Head Start, the Job Corps, VISTA, OEO and Legal Services to the Poor—all those genuine commitments of really effective service to the poor that we were once so proud of.

Looking back on all this, I have often wished that I could bring a group together to develop alternatives to the blind military force which seems to be the only way we can imagine to address our terrorist threats today. We have to put a new face on the image of the United States in the Arab and Muslim world, and elsewhere as well, because our credibility as a force for peace is fast declining all around the world.

As we celebrate fifty years since the War on Poverty began, we need some imagination on programs for human and social development in our time that could parallel the visionary energy that we once saw in the days of Kennedy and Johnson and Shriver. And in our foreign policy, creating fear of our exceptionalist Empire seems to be our only trumpet call, and we have to get back to leading the world in hope.

That summer I went to Philadelphia for the funeral of the last of my siblings, my older sister, Agnes Marie. I now found myself the lone rider—as I still am ten years later— of our original family of seven, my parents and the five of us children. I am still deeply aware of how that painful reality continues to shape how I listen to the stories of others who have had a less turbulent family history.

Donna and I later drove with fellow Pilgrim Gene Boutilier and a few other residents to Nevada on November 1-3, 2004, to monitor presidential polling places in Las Vegas. We were trained by Election Protection, a national coalition led by People for the American Way. There had been a history of people of color being pushed away in Las Vegas, and we found that the personal support we could give to Blacks and Latinos in their right to vote was very satisfying. It was a challenging day full of energy and hope.

We then went on to British Columbia, where we met with a mysterious separatist sect of radical pacifists from Russia, called the Doukhobors, and I also gave an address at a wonderful Fellowship of Reconciliation meeting there. Donna finished her term on the California Senior Legislature, and happily saw the bill she had introduced on nursing home residents' rights get enacted into California law.

She then began serving on the Board of Directors for Pilgrim Place, with all its related meetings and committee work. One of her most important ventures was beginning a Task Force to explore creative options for long term care around here, and that still remains one of her priorities.

Donna was appointed to the National Consumer Advocacy Board of the Medicare Rights Center, and she wrote a series of newspaper articles giving a critical analysis of the new Medicare drug benefit law.

She has been remarkably faithful to her strong exercise regime—Yoga, Tai Chi, Qi Gong, water aerobics, working out on our exercise machines—and some chronic back pain that had been with her for almost thirty years is now considerably better. Her commitment to keeping herself in shape drives me to keep up with her when I feel weakest, and I'm grateful for that.

Vietnam, Bangkok and Cambodia

2005 began with a three-week trip to Vietnam, Bangkok in Thailand, and the shimmering temples of Angkor Wat in Cambodia. It was a wonderful, if strenuous, plunge into a part of the world where we had never been. We celebrated my 75th birthday in an open longboat putt-putting up a narrow jungle river in the Mekong Delta, expecting any minute to meet a Viet Cong militiaman around the next bend.

We were just twelve people, in a group led by Overseas Adventure Travel, and as we came down the whole country from Hanoi to Ho Chi Minh City (Saigon), we were able to speak with many people, even visiting for dinner in several homes. We were very impressed at how comfortable and content they seemed around their warm and very simple tables.

Continually, they said that they are a Buddhist people, with no urge for an eye-for-an-eye and a tooth-for-a-tooth. They have just moved on and welcome Americans with great warmth. Rather awesome, and I'm still digesting all of that. An insightful and well-travelled Maryknoll priest whom we met in Bangkok wryly remarked that we might not find such peaceable tolerance in the Muslim culture when we finish with our devastation in Iraq.

Our rich visit to Vietnam was a quiet, searching pilgrimage for me. It helped me stay centered as I grappled with my own shame and anger at what we were doing in Iraq and the arrogant violence of the American Empire around the world. I wanted to ask ordinary Vietnamese how they handle their angers about what my country has done to them, and to their land, which is still recovering from the Agent Orange and napalm wasteland that we have made of much of it.

I began speaking to groups of all kinds, two or three a month, this time on "Creative Peacemaking: What if we brought our troops home, now?" And I was invited to speak on U.S. National Security and the Global Empire at a major World Peace Forum in Vancouver in June.

We didn't quite "bring the troops home" from Iraq but it was still good work, and the call remains as vital even today. In the summer, we went off to Sedona, Arizona, to wonder at the marvelous red-rock beauty of the quiet, rolling desert, and that quieted my soul a bit.

The death penalty was also a major focus for me that year, as it still continues to be. In December, a quiet group of us at Pilgrim Place held a candlelight vigil at midnight around our flagpole as a protest against the execution of a man named Stanley Tookie Williams at San Quentin.

But our Governor, Arnold Schwarzenegger the Terminator, lived up to his name and sadly missed a splendid opportunity for moral leadership. And we all suffered a great loss, in the name of a barbaric system of eye-for-an-eye vengeance calling itself justice.

I also returned to the Board of Progressive Christians Uniting, the dynamic and interdenominational group that had nourished and supported my social justice commitments for so many years. It took lots of time and energy, but it was, as always, good work.

A major crisis that year was when the IRS threatened to revoke the tax-exempt status of All Saints Episcopal Church in Pasadena which, along with Pilgrim Place, had been our primary Christian community for ten years, as it remains today.

The IRS cited an anti-war sermon of our former Rector, George Regas, just prior to the 2004 election, claiming it was a partisan political speech. However, at no point had George ever told anyone to vote for any candidate. Rather, he challenged both candidates to reexamine their support for the preemptive war in Iraq in the light of Christian teaching.

There were major issues of religious freedom and freedom of speech here, as well as our urgent need to bring the dreadful war in Iraq to an end. Although the threatened lawsuit cost All Saints a great deal of money, our attorneys won our case. It became a bright statement that All Saints is indeed a peace church, and we got dozens of new members to help us with the costs of this outrage. Once an old woman came into the church and said, "I don't believe in God, but if I did, I'd be a member at All Saints." We began to chant, "The IRS is welcome in our pews, but not in our pulpit."

Out of the Forests of Paraguay

Our major adventure of 2006 began with a week-long visit in February to the World Council of Churches Assembly in Porto Alegre, Brazil. As I have mentioned, I had been to Porto Alegre several years earlier for the World Social Forum, and it was great to be back there for another international gathering dedicated to peace and justice.

We then went for two weeks to Paraguay—with a brief stop in Argentina, where we were thrilled by the awesome Iguassu Falls, one of the largest waterfalls in the world. We travelled with an international group of twelve led by English journalist Margaret Hebblethwaite, to visit some of the thirty villages that were missions of the early Spanish Jesuits with the Guarani Indians in the seventeenth and eighteenth centuries, known as the "Reductions." These lay on the borders of Paraguay, Brazil and Argentina, and they were fantastic Christian Socialist experiments, among the greatest examples of creative Liberation Theology, celebrated even today.

In 1767, after 150 years of missionary development and empowerment, the whole Guarani Nation, along with their brave Jesuit protectors, was violently trampled and dispersed by the ruthless Spanish and Portuguese Conquistadores, who hated the Jesuits for saving the Guarani from becoming colonial slaves in their mines. It was a terrible massacre by the colonial overlords.

Having first heard of all this in my earliest years as a Jesuit sixty years earlier, I was profoundly moved to stand in the footsteps and shadowy ruins of what those great men had helped the Indians build, and to try to imagine what it must have been like for a young Spanish Jesuit, in 1609, to head out into the vast Paraguayan forest, alone or with a few others, and with little means of contact back home, half a world away. This is the story so powerfully told in the Robert de Niro and Jeremy Irons film "The Mission," and I still thrill to it. In 2006, the *New York Times* did a wonderful job describing it all in a three-page picture spread called "Missions of a Lost Utopia."

In the final week of that great adventure, while hiking in the cloudy forests in Paraguay and sitting on a great log, I was bitten by a red ant or a scorpion and contracted what was later diagnosed as a severe pepto-streptococcal infection. That became a life-changing event for me. And in many ways for Donna as well.

On our return home in early March, I was taken immediately to the hospital in Pomona. I had three surgeries to remove lots of gangrene and horrific infectious tissue and I was in bed for ten weeks, first in the hospital, then in the Health Center and at home in Pilgrim Place. I lost thirty-five pounds in the first thirty-five days, due to heavy antibiotics and appetite loss, and I was out of circulation for nearly nine months.

In all that time, besides my dear Donna and devoted Pilgrim friends, I was splendidly cared for by Visiting Nurses, remarkable women who appeared daily at my bedside to change the dressings on my surgical wounds and to nurture my spirit in the long, dark tunnel until I could get to physical therapy.

Chief among the angels around my bed was a wonderful VNA Nurse, Sharon Berry, who was later named our Director of Wellness and Clinical Services at Pilgrim Place. I have always been honored that I had the privilege of first recommending Sharon for that position, and I don't know what I would have ever done without her priestly hands of healing through my various creaky times since then.

One of our chief gifts in all that time was the overwhelming support we received from this dear community at Pilgrim Place. Friends here organized small teams to try to encourage me to eat during my time of extraordinary loss of weight and appetite.

A very dear 92-year old friend made her special soup for me, friends came to sit with me, and resident harpists played for me. There were phone calls, visits from family and friends from afar, CDs and books and meals for me. I'm still deeply moved to hear people recall the whole experience even today, and we are aware of all that we have to be grateful for.

It was an all-engrossing physical and spiritual journey, and I was for some weeks very close to the edge of the abyss, in a way that I was too weak to realize. Donna did realize that, of course, and she was dearer to me than ever before in our then thirty-seven wonderful years together.

We each learned that our relationship had moved into a deeper place in that very tense time together, and we praised the Lord for it. We both had pledged long ago to be caregivers, of course, to take care of each other for better or for worse until death do us part. But this time, we were each just desperate enough and just powerless enough that we moved beyond being caregivers to being more deeply lovers.

Several major insights still keep coming forward from that near-death experience, from which I still have not completely recovered. Most of all, I have a new awareness of being vulnerable. No matter how much I feel in control of my world, macho that I think I am, I am altogether fragile and radically dependent in body and spirit, needing to be in community and to trust in others in order to be myself.

My awareness of being alone on the edge of the abyss, of being unable to save or heal myself, led me to let go of myself and give myself over to the healing forces of the universe, and specifically into the arms of the Risen Christ.

Night after night, when all was quiet around my bed, a fading image repeatedly came to me in the dim light of my sickroom ceiling. I recognized myself lying wrapped in a dark burial shroud and floating motionless and peacefully in the emptiness above me. But, through the fogginess of my spirit, I somehow knew that, in the words of the old revival hymn, "Leaning, leaning on the everlasting arms," I was indeed "safe and secure from all alarms."

This sense of needing to be in community has led me to a new awareness of the call to compassion in my life. Compassion is the fundamental building block of all community, and the Christian life could be described as a journey into compassion. Several of those around my bed, including especially my Donna, epitomized this for me.

I remember once telling one of my very special nurses in the hospital: "You are really more than a care-giver to me. You give me all the medical care I need, and you're a real professional at that. But I feel that you are also entering deeply into my healing process with all your heart and your spirit, and that is therapeutic in itself." She began to softly cry, and said, "That's why I became a nurse."

I shall always be grateful for the compassionate touch and loving presence of so many nurses on this journey, and I salute them for what I call their priestly hands of healing in a world of so much pain.

I also sense a new gentleness in myself, a need to express my tenderness and my loving care for others. This is a deeply emotional challenge, rather complex and difficult to describe, but I'm very conscious of trying to respond to its call.

When I told her about this new sensitivity to express-ing tenderness, my warmly intuitive friend, Wendy Bayer, suggested that I'm just getting more deeply in touch

with my own feminine self. And I suddenly realized
that for almost ten months, a very long time, I had been
surrounded almost exclusively by loving women touching and caring for me. This is still a very rich time in
the center of my spirit, well worth all the pain and the
darkness that has made it possible. I only hope I can be
worthy of it.

In all of this time, Donna was sending regular reports
of the ups and downs of my progress to all of our friends.
My near-death experience was obviously a monumental
turning point in our lives, and we shared it as best we
could with friends far and near. We still cherish a large
file of the hundreds of emotional letters we received from
relatives and dear friends at Pilgrim Place and from literally all around the world. I've recently read through every
one of them again, and their warm love and caring, their
genuine compassion, remains a splendid blessing for
which I am grateful beyond the singing of it.

Teilhard de Chardin

My French Jesuit brother, Pierre Teilhard de Chardin,
a paleontologist, theologian, and seer, has offered me
special vision and energy on this journey. His books,
The Phenomenon of Man and *The Divine Milieu*, are
important milestones in the history of Western thought.
He is one of the great gurus of my life.

Years ago, when I was still a promising young man
and not at all concerned about growing old, I remember
being deeply moved by Teilhard's poetic reflections on

growing old and on dying, in *The Divine Milieu*. I have often gone back to those reflections, and they have become the theological and spiritual synthesis of all that I would hope to take away with me as I move into this new and precious season of my life.

Teilhard's international renown as a paleontologist made him particularly aware of the unity of all things in Christ. And to be aware of that unity, he says, is to be aware that, in the first half of our lives, we must "divinize our activities," become one with the redeeming Christ in all that we do. In the second half of our lives, he says, our call is to "hallow our diminishments," learn to sanctify our "passivities."

Hallowing is a wonderful word. It means "to make holy, to consecrate." A secondary meaning is "to respect greatly, to venerate." Teilhard discusses the various diminishments which we experience, those things that gradually fade from our grasp as we grow older. Among them are: 1) The loss of persons dear to us. 2) The loss of our traditional persona, the identity that has made us who we are before others. 3) The gradual dimming or loss of our physical and mental powers. And, finally, the ultimate diminishment that is death.

Teilhard says that the key to learning to hallow my progressive diminishments lies in a profound and deeply spiritual level of acceptance—a positive claiming of them, even honoring them as my own. It is only then that something creative can be made of them. To treat the diminishment as a companion, so that I can afford a certain detachment toward it, with even a kind of playfulness.

According to Teilhard, the final hallowing of all diminishments, including death, lies in seeking to make them a means of communion with God. "Communion through diminishment" is his term. In a splendid conclusion to *The Divine Milieu*, he moves from closely reasoned exposition to the poetry of prayer:

> Grant that I may willingly consent to this phase of communion, in the course of which I shall possess you by diminishing in you.
>
> When the signs of age begin to mark my body (and still more when they touch my mind); when the ill that is to diminish me or carry me off strikes from without or is born within me; when the painful moment comes in which I suddenly awaken to the fact that I am ill or growing old; and, above all, at that last moment when I feel that I am losing hold of myself and am absolutely passive within the hands of the great unknown forces that have formed me; in all those dark moments, O God, grant that I may understand that it is you who is painfully parting the fibers of my being in order to penetrate to the very marrow of my substance and bear me away within yourself.

I have had a wonderful reception to a Vespers talk which I gave twice at Pilgrim Place, in 1999 and again in 2010, on "Hallowing Our Diminishments," and Teilhard's vision still vibrates deep in my heart.

While still recovering in 2006-7 from that awesome bite in Paraguay, I got deeply immersed in Process Theology, first brought to my attention by the splendid work of our renowned resident theologian, John Cobb.

I wondered why it had taken me so long to get to Process Thought. It opened up a whole new theological horizon, and the seasons of my faith were leading me beyond the religion of creed and doctrine and moral edicts, even if all that had served me well in an earlier season of my faith.

In my current search for the "emerging" church, Process Thought speaks to my commitment to a Rahnerian incarnational theology, and it also rings echoes in me of my Latin American Liberation Theology. It remains a challenging venture for me, and I hear still further echoes of it today with my recent opening to Buddhist thought. What goes round comes round, and the glittering synthesis of it all can be very stimulating.

It will be a great challenge to probe what being a Buddha Christian might involve at this stage in my journey. There is a lot of wonderful reading that lies ahead here, and I look to my growing number of Buddhist friends at Pilgrim Place for all the help I need. I already see how my initial Buddhist thinking has affected how I experience sacramental signs in the Christian liturgy, and I have a new edge and depth as I worship now.

When my body had somewhat healed, I slowly started out on the peace and justice circuit again, and that felt like good work, even as I was outraged and depressed at the ferocious destruction being wrought by the American Empire, and by the ruthless mindlessness of our interventionist President, George W. Bush.

I was invited to serve on the National Board of the Fellowship of Reconciliation, but concluded that my strength was too diminished for quarterly weekend trips to Nyack, New York, and so I had to decline that call with great regret. However, it was still manageable to continue on the Board of Progressive Christians Uniting, which was now expanding beyond Southern California, and that was very fulfilling.

The Terrible Tears of the World

A major event of 2007 was the death of B. Davie Napier, my guru and one of my dearest friends in all the world. Davie had preceded me with great acclaim as Dean of the Chapel at Stanford many years earlier. He had taught me a great deal, and he and his wonderful wife, Joy, were key to our coming to Pilgrim Place in 1996. I remember that Davie and Joy had urged Donna and me, when we were first looking over Pilgrim Place, to "Come earlier than later, and grow old together with us." Deeply moved, we did that, and it was one of the best decisions we ever made.

We were at Davie's bedside as he drew his last breath, Donna reading aloud from his wonderful book, "Come,

Sweet Death." I asked him if he had any last word for me, and he said: "Thomas, my brother, *keep working to stop the terrible tears of the world.*" I bear that mantra and that mission deep in my heart to this day.

This is why the terrible tears of those crying little children in their diapers and bare feet and hungry swollen bellies which we keep seeing in the deserts of the world, why all this is so urgent in my spirit. It keeps me searching and listening for some place where I might somehow come to them to help them dry their tears.

I saw them in South Africa and I've seen them all over Central America, and I've seen them in the West Bank and Gaza. I see them today in rural Mississippi and Los Angeles. And I know that they are also here in Claremont, although I haven't ever had a chance to touch into their world.

I am always in search for where the valuable place might be for this 84 year-old in the midst of such terrible tears and the outrageous political abuse that prevents a world of peace and justice from ever coming true. Liturgy is not three feet off the ground in some *Neverland* of cuddling up to my own little Jesus, but it is the absolute energy and nourishment I need to go to work in the world to make it a better place. And this is why the weekly Eucharist, both here and at All Saints, is so very important for me. I always come away feeling deeply nourished by being at that table, and I find that I simply can't do without it.

In 2008, Sharon Berry finally arrived as Clinic Nurse at Pilgrim Place, and she came just in time to help me with a Stage 3 Melanoma which was found on my back. Sharon has been an angel of mercy at Pilgrim Place, and her priestly hands of healing are a marvelous grace for us all.

I completed my tenth and final year on the Board of Progressive Christians Uniting and wished them well. The election of Barack Obama was a blessing beyond compare for the world that year, and a balm for my bruised political soul. I felt we just might have a Leader in the White House, at last.

At All Saints Church, Pasadena, 2007

At the time, I was being fed by the work of Andrew Bacevich in his new book, *The Limits of Power: The End of American Exceptionalism*. It is a powerful and depressing critique of the U.S. Empire in the world today, leaning strongly on Reinhold Niebuhr for his analysis of the political world of the 1990s.

I saw in Barack Obama the promise of a new foreign policy that moves toward peacemaking and diplomatic problem solving, interdependence and work for the common good. Despite some later bumps in his road, I still see that promise in Obama, and we have to work with him to make it happen.

The Later Years For Now

In the years which have followed, my passions remain focused on Israel and Palestine, South Africa, Central America, the Middle East and Iraq. Daily listservs from Israel and the West Bank keep me angry, wondering how to react with any wisdom. And I began writing these memoirs with the wonderful help of a great friend of many long years, John Morearty.

John had a radio talk show in Stockton, and he insisted on coming down here to interview me for his show and to urgently get me started on my writing. John died last year, and I'm still very grateful to him for the nudge that he gave me, among so many other of his blessings over the years.

I became deeply enthused and involved with "Occupy Wall Street," which I find one of the most promising political movements of our time. Its cry that "We are the 99%" and its focus on the vast income differences between rich and poor in our country have made a real difference in our national discussion; and a group of us at Pilgrim Place issued a "Statement of Conscience from a Community of Elders with the 99%," which got some initial response from churches in the area.

As never before, both the 99% and the 1% are being challenged to talk about the yawning gap between the rich and everyone else in our society, and we have Occupy to thank for sowing those seeds. Some wizards in the media are wondering what has happened to the Occupy movement, since it doesn't seem to have any tangible shape or leadership any more.

But Occupy intentionally began very low to the ground, and it has raised critically important issues of economic justice all over the country. These will continue to be with us, however long the actual movement remains visible. I am urging us all to just praise the Lord for that, and get on with the work.

A couple of years ago I thoroughly enjoyed a three-day environmental conference here, led by Bill McKibben, called "Brave New Planet." At the time, I was looking deeply into the interplay between patriotism and environmentalism, and I gave a paper at the McKibben conference that was entitled "Politics and Patriotism on a Brave New Planet." And I still continue to work as best I can on environmental issues and Earth Warming.

I have been deeply moved recently by Lester Brown's story of his life, *Breaking New Ground: A Personal History*.

Lester Brown has been called "one of the world's most influential thinkers," and the "guru of the environmental movement."

His book *Plan B 4.0: Mobilizing to Save Civilization* lays out more than you may care to know about the dying of our planet, but then he goes on to concretely describe some things which you and I might do about it. Lester Brown's Worldwatch Institute and Earth Policy Institute have done remarkable work on an environmentally sustainable economy.

But the rich humanity of the man himself is what has really capitivated me. Lester Brown was born of dirt-farmers in New Jersey who couldn't read. He was the youngest of three children, and he was the first in his family to get through the eighth grade. He earned three graduate degrees and wrote 50 books published in 43 languages.

Now retired, Brown lives in a simple one-bedroom apartment in Rock Creek Park in Washington, just down from the Zoo, where he says he can hear the lions roar. He has no car, and has turned over all of his very significant income to the organizations he has served, living only on the savings he needs to sustain himself. Lester Brown not only talks the talk, but he walks the walk, and he's an enormous inspiration to me.

Meanwhile, Donna and I have been giving lots of time to important family issues. Our niece, Shana Ogren, has recovered slowly from being thrown from a pick-up truck while a Peace Corps Volunteer in Malawi. She is a great heroine of ours, and she has just given birth to her second child. Praise the Lord for her fine healing.

In 2008, Quentin "Bud" Ogren, Donna's brother-in-law, died at ninety-three in San Luis Obispo. He had a dynamic singing voice, and he always made it to any piano in sight. His last words to a family throng around his bed were, "I'm stickin' to the union 'til the day I die."

His father had been the Socialist candidate for Mayor in Rockford, Illinois, and he had met Donna's sister, Paula, at a national Young People's Socialist League (YPSL) Conference in New York. They married in 1940 and had seven children, one of whom died very young.

Bud Ogren was a dynamic labor lawyer and a constitutional law professor for thirty-two years at Loyola Law School in Los Angeles. Earlier, he had worked for the National Labor Relations Board, and, among his other challenging ventures, he was once director of Mortimer Adler's Great Books Program in Southern California.

Paula was ten years older than Donna, and had an IQ of 176. She was a real polymath, and one year in the 1970s she was Champion of Champions on Jeopardy. Like Donna, she had two Master's Degrees and became a lawyer at age sixty-two, not wanting to be outdone by her little sister.

Paula taught history at a Catholic boys high school in Watts, and later worked as a public defender, mainly assisting juvenile offenders in Los Angeles. She died in August, 2010, at age ninety-one also surrounded by a throng of dynamic children and grandchildren.

Among the things left in Paula and Bud's home after their death were at least ten thousand books, and, along with the piles of newspapers to which they subscribed, it often looked like a local branch of the Public Library. We remember many a roaring family reunion in that vivacious home.

Three weeks earlier than Paula, our nephew Paul Ogren's dear wife, Sandra Gardebring, died. She had been a Justice on the Minnesota Supreme Court, and was Vice President at Cal Poly San Luis Obispo when she died of a rare cancer at the age of 63. Beautiful memorial services for three magnificent people!

And then, in April of 2012, a very specially dear friend to many of us here at Pilgrim Place died. Joann Lamb was a superb model of deep spirituality with a lifelong active commitment to peace and justice. She was always active in the Grail, and we were continually inspired by her joyous, gentle presence, her abundant acts of loving kindness, her energy and her generosity of spirit.

With her husband, Jim, also our very dear friend, Joann was deeply involved in peace and justice work around the world, and especially in Mexico; and her lovely family of children and grandchildren are still a warm and inspiring delight to me as they come to visit us. I have pictures of them all over my wall here as I write. We praise the Lord for the shining and gracious spirit of Joann Lamb, which still lives vitally among us.

We moved to our new apartment in Friendship Court in 2011, part of our Assisted Living unit at Pilgrim Place. It is warm and has 850 square feet of bright open space, but that is about half of what we had lived in for the previous fifteen years and not enough for two separate offices. We have, however, two spacious bedrooms, and my corner desk in one of them is where, as I tell Donna, *"all the big ideas are thought."* It is from there that these immortal words have been emerging.

I had the first of a series of falls back in 2009, bringing an ambulance to weave its way silently through the curious Pilgrim Place Festival crowds. I then took four more bad falls at the end of 2012, leaving me with a compression fracture in my spine. Heavy radiation for some prostate cancer also continues to keep me rather weak. I haven't really recovered from it all, and it still takes me time to get around. That probably means an end to very much physical travel on my journey now. But all in all, this Elder is really in rather good health, and still travelling gently on my spiritual journey, praise the Lord!

Postlude and Epilogue

So here is the tale of my now 84 years. When I look at how my personal theology and spirituality have evolved along the stages of this priestly pilgrimage, I can discern several major expanding circles. But central to all these circles is the fact that I have always chosen to live on the fringe, on the pilgrim road, in between institutions.

In many of the life-changing career decisions which I have made, I have been a lone rider making my way over priestly ground that often had not yet been broken. I have always felt myself "riding my saddle lightly" in the institutional Church. In fact, I see now that I was, from the beginning, always growing toward my "season" of leaving Church, always searching for new ways to be priestly person and to uncover the risen Christ in the world.

I have already mentioned that little story about Bishop Hannan and his very troubling parish renegades who wanted, of all things, to have Bible study in Scranton parishes. Nothing could make clearer the fact that, to Catholics for generations before Vatican II, "The Church" meant the Roman Catholic Church, and that Church was frequently equated with the hierarchy.

As I went off to the Jesuits in the 1940s, Catholicism was highly cultic, with a view of a priest as a man above others, a man with semi-divine powers. The clerical wagons were in a tight circle, with little room for critique of the church and its teachings and with serious doubt about any salvation outside it.

Pieces of that clerical structure, but certainly not all of it, have cracked away since Vatican II, but I am somehow a child of it still, and I carry lasting marks from it on my soul. And it is that ponderous and clerical "Church" which I have long ago left behind, without having at all left the true church as the beloved Christian community.

So I am pilgrim on the road, a transdenominational Christian with roots in the Roman Catholic tradition and always in search of the Beloved Community. And in the fresh reality of myself as priestly person, I am still driven by a clarion call to find the valuable place for me to be.

Not just any place, but a place where I can do good work, work that really makes a difference in drying the terrible tears, and where, as Frederick Buechner so beautifully puts it, "my deep gladness meets the world's deep hunger."

The priestly journey goes on. A great theme which keeps me going is "If you want to have an interesting life, make a lot of decisions. If you make a wrong one, make another." Oscar Wilde also intrigued me once when he said, "Be yourself. Everyone else is already taken."

And I am deeply nourished by the words of Archbishop Romero of El Salvador. "Try not to depend on hope," he said, "because unfulfilled hope leads to despair. Try instead to be faithful." I am just trying to be faithful every morning, to see what creative love I can bring to this day ahead of me, for the possibilities of new life for all the sisters and all the brothers around and beyond me in all the world.

January 2014

Thank you for your patience with all this, and I'd be glad to hear from you if you're ever so moved. You'll find me, God willing, at 627 Leyden Lane, Claremont, CA 91711, or at *tambrogi@verizon.net*, or at 909.625.2558. Go well and stay well on your own journeys.

Some Authors I Have Loved

Bacevich, Andrew, *The Limits of Power: The End of American Exceptionalism.* Macmillan, 2008.

Berger, Peter, *A Rumor of Angels: Modern Society and the Rediscovery of the Supernatural.* Anchor, 1970.

Brown, Lester, *Plan B 4.0: Mobilizing to Save Civilization.* Norton, 2012.

Brown, Lester, *Breaking New Ground: A Personal History.* Norton, 2013.

Brown, Robert McAfee, *Reflections Over the Long Haul: A Memoir.* Westminster, 2005.

Gutierrez, Gustavo, *A Theology of Liberation: History, Politics and Salvation.* Orbis, 1971.

Knitter, Paul, *Without Buddha I Could Not Be A Christian.* Oneworld Publications, 2009.

Lappé, Frances Moore, *Diet for a Small Planet.* Ballantine, 1985.

O'Brien, Niall, *Revolution From The Heart.* Oxford, 1987.

Rahner, Karl, *Encounters With Silence.* Newman Press, 1960.

Schell, Jonathan, *The Unconquerable World: Power, Non-Violence and the Will of the People.* Holt, 2003.

Stiglitz, Joseph and Linda Bilmes, *The Three Trillion Dollar War: The True Cost of the Iraq Conflict.* Norton, 2008.

Teilhard de Chardin, Pierre, *Le Milieu Divin: An Essay on the Interior Life.* Fontana, 1978.